JOHN DEVANEY

BART STARR

COVER/ASARO

SBS SCHOLASTIC BOOK SERVICES
New York • London • Richmond Hill, Ontario

TO MY FATHER

Copyright © 1967 by Scholastic Magazines, Inc. All rights reserved. Published by Scholastic Book Services, a division of Scholastic Magazines, Inc.

1st printing .... September 1967

Printed in the U.S.A.

CONTENTS

1. Bart the Cool 5
2. What Bart Starr Is Really Like 15
3. High School Quarterback 25
4. The Came the Miseries 33
5. Vince Needs a Quarterback 41
6. Bart Starr — A Failure 50
7. Victoryl 58
8. "We Had It in our Hearts" 71
9. A Day in the Lions' Den 82
10. Who Is Better — Unitas or Starr? 93
11. How to Be a Winning Quarterback . . 101
12. Bart Starr at Home: "Not a Mean
    Word" 112
13. The Only Place To Be 119
14. "A Success at Anything in Life" 132
Appendix:
    Highlights of Bart Starr's Career 142

Illustrations appear between pages 72 and 73.

1

Bart the Cool

THE PLACE: THE SUPER
Bowl. The date: January 15, 1967. Millions are
watching on television across the country. Inside
the Los Angeles Coliseum some sixty-three thousand fans are standing, screaming, as Bart Starr
drops back to pass. He looks to his right, sees Max
McGee, and throws, but the ball sails ten feet
over McGee's head.

Fans of the Kansas City Chiefs, watching from
the stands, roar with delight. "Starr is cracking
up!" yells one Kansas City fan. "He can't take a
tough pass rush. Today he's going to collapse
under the toughest pass rush of his life!"

Moments later the big Kansas City tackle,
Buck Buchanan, bursts by a Green Bay blocker
and slams Starr to the ground. Starr gets up
slowly.

On the next play as Starr takes the snap from
center and again fades back to pass, two Kansas
City linemen thunder down on him. *Smack!*
Down goes Starr for a five-yard loss, buried
under a quarter-ton of muscle and bone.

The six-foot, two-hundred-pound Starr pulls
himself up from the grass, flips the ball to the

referee, and trots slowly toward the sideline. In comes the Green Bay punting unit, for it is now fourth down and long yardage to go. Starr trots off the field as he always does, arms flapping loosely at his sides, on his face the calm expression of a man doing arithmetic in his head.

The Kansas City fans roar with delight. "This," they are saying, "this is going to be the worst day of Bart Starr's life . . ."

This warm and hazy day should have been one of the biggest days in Bart Starr's life. Here he was, leading the National Football League champions, the Green Bay Packers, into the first Super Bowl to play the American Football League champions, the Kansas City Chiefs. For years pro-football fans had argued: Which is the better league — the American Football League or the National Football League?

Early in 1966 the two leagues had at last agreed to match their champions against each other in a Super Bowl game. Now, today, on this field, the argument would be decided.

The National Football League was the older league, the American Football League a five-year-old upstart. Ever since the AFL began, NFL fans had pointed to the Green Bay Packers and said: "The AFL has no team like this." And they had pointed to Bart Starr and said: "The AFL has no quarterback like this."

Now, today, on this field, Bart Starr and the Packers would have to prove true the boasts of their fans. If the Packers failed and the Chiefs won, Starr and the Packers would leave Los Angeles humiliated, laughed at, and scorned — branded fake champions.

Down at the Packer bench, Starr fixed a pair of headphones to his ears. He began to speak through a small microphone to a coach high in a booth above the stadium. The coach was telling Starr how the Chief linemen were crashing through to knock him down when he tried to pass.

"Yes," said Starr, speaking in a soft Alabama drawl. "Yes, I saw that they were doing that. Maybe we can throw passes in that direction. They've left themselves open, I think, on the right."

The coach's voice crackled over the earphones. Starr listened, nodding, then said, "OK, we'll try it."

He took off the earphones, handing them to the Packers' No. Two quarterback, Bart's close friend, Zeke Bratkowski. Starr's blue eyes stared out at the field.

Bart Starr, they say in the NFL, is cool. He works in a cool, methodical way, usually moving his team toward the goal line in short bursts. He does not rattle easily — though there was a time when he did. Today he had the chance to show just how cool he could be. On this day of days, with tension inside each player, would tension jerk Bart Starr's passes off their target?

A minute later he trotted back onto the field. The Kansas City fans chanted: "Throw him back, throw him back."

Starr ducked into the Packer huddle. The ball rested on the Green Bay twenty-yard line, a long eighty yards away from the Chiefs' end zone.

Out of the huddle trotted the Packers. Center Bob Curry slapped a pair of big hands around the ball, crouching to snap it back to Starr. Starr, hands on hips, was scanning the Chiefs' defense, looking for a weakness.

Now, like the burst of a machine gun, Starr was rattling out the signals: "Ninety-eight . . . red . . . thirty-five . . ."

Starr took the snap, wheeled with the grace of a bullfighter, and handed the ball to halfback Elijah Pitts. The slim-hipped Pitts danced through a hole for a three-yard gain.

It was second down and seven yards to go, the ball on the Green Bay twenty-three. In the huddle, remembering what the assistant coach had told him on the phone, Starr called for a pass to the right.

He took the snap and raced back into the cup of blockers, looking coolly for a receiver. He saw end Marv Fleming running across the middle. *Zip!* Starr flashed the ball on a line and it thumped into Fleming's chest. The big end grabbed the ball and toppled to the ground.

First down for the Packers! The ball was on the Green Bay thirty-four. "Get Starr!" the Chief fans were yelling. "Knock down Starr!"

On the next play big Buck Buchanan blasted by a Green Bay blocker, arms outstretched to hammer down Starr. Bart ducked, the lineman flashing by him. Then Starr threw a line-drive pass that Pitts caught on the Kansas City forty-four.

Another first down! The ball rested on the grass some forty-four yards from the end zone. Two plays later the Packers had pushed the ball to the thirty-seven, and now it was third down and three yards to go for a first down.

Third down! Three yards to go! Those are the cruelest words a quarterback can hear. Your last

chance to get a first down. *Three yards to go!*
A lot of yardage when a defense tightens up to
stop you.

Starr crouched inside the huddle, talking
quickly and emphatically to the Packers. "When
you call a play," he once said, "have confidence
in your voice. You may have doubt about the
play, but you don't want your team to have that
doubt. You've got to sound like a marine sergeant
out there, barking out the plays. If the players
have confidence in the play . . . you can make
the worst play work."

As he barked out this play, Starr had confidence it would work. In the week before this
game, he had studied films of the Kansas City
defense. And, watching, he had seen mistakes.
Now, methodically, he would try to take advantage of those mistakes.

Starr took the snap and faded back. His end,
Max McGee, veered toward a Kansas City halfback. The halfback jumped in front of Max, and
that was the mistake Starr hoped to see.

McGee cut back toward the middle of the
field, five yards ahead of the surprised halfback.
Starr lined a pass that McGee cradled to his chest
on the fifteen-yard line. Then, the halfback
straining behind him, McGee sprinted into the
end zone. Moments later Green Bay booted the
extra point and led, 7-0.

Kansas City, the pride of the AFL, didn't quit.
With quarterback Lenny Dawson throwing beautiful spiral passes, the Chiefs marched down the
field to tie the score, 7-7.

After the kickoff, Starr steered the Packers to
their own forty-two. Two plays failed to gain.
Again it was third down and ten yards to go. The

Chiefs knew what Starr had to do: He had to pass.

The Chiefs dropped back to bat down the pass, but Bart threaded a pass through the Chief defense into the hands of Carroll Dale, who leaped high to snare the ball on the Kansas City forty-three.

A minute later the Packers stood on the Kansas City thirty-eight, third down and five yards to go. In the stands the Green Bay rooters twisted programs in wet hands and wondered: Was it possible that Starr would come through with another clutch play on third down?

Starr faded back and threw a looping pass toward the right sideline. There end Marv Fleming raced under the ball and pulled it to his chest for a first down on the Chiefs' twenty-seven-yard line.

Two plays later the Packers had pushed to the twenty-four. It was third down and seven yards to go. *Another big third-down play for Starr!* "Stop him!" yelled the Chief rooters. "Stop Starr!"

Again Starr faded to pass. He threw a quick pass to Elijah Pitts, and the halfback twisted to the fourteen. From there fullback Jim Taylor carried the ball around left end and into the end zone. Now the Packers led, 14-7.

The Chiefs clawed back, pushing toward the Green Bay goal line. Stopped short of the end zone by the burly Green Bay defense, the Chiefs kicked a thirty-four-yard field goal. Minutes later a gun barked, ending the first half with the score Green Bay 14, Kansas City 10.

All across the country people got up from their TV sets and said: "Starr has been magnificent, but Kansas City, it won't give up."

"We'll win! We'll win! We'll win!" chanted the Chiefs' rooters in the stands at the Coliseum. "We're close enough to win!"

In the Green Bay clubhouse, assistant coaches pulled up stools next to Starr. Pointing to their charts, they talked to him about the Kansas City defense. "You're doing just what our game plan called for," a coach said to Starr. "If we can keep fooling those cornerbacks with those passes, we're good for another couple of TDs."

Starr nodded. Then he asked questions, quickly and directly, no excitement in his voice. He could have been a stranger asking directions in a foreign city. The coaches answered his questions. Starr listened, quiet and attentive.

Out ran the two teams for the start of the second half, the Coliseum a big bowl filled with the crowd's roaring. On the fourth play of the half, Lenny Dawson faded to pass. Rushed, he threw a soft floater that Green Bay's Willie Wood intercepted on the Packer forty-five. Protected by a screen of blockers, Wood skipped down the sideline all the way to the Kansas City five. From there Starr handed off to Pitts, who thrust over left tackle to score. Now Green Bay led, 21-10.

"Keep up the pressure!" yelled coach Vince Lombardi as the exultant Packers came back to the bench. "They're still close. We got to get on that scoreboard again."

Bart Starr nodded, the face still calm. He was still Bart the Cool in moments like this, when the game was going well for him, just as he had been Bart the Cool when the game had been going badly for him.

A little later the Packers drove to the Kansas

City forty-four: Third down, eleven yards to go.
Another tough third-down situation.

Starr stepped back to pass. In rushed the big
Kansas City defensemen. Calmly, Starr whisked
a pass some twenty yards downfield, where two
defenders were converging on Max McGee.
The pass shot between the two defenders,
McGee clutching the ball on the Chiefs' twenty-
eight. Green Bay had another first down.

Moments later Starr told McGee to run the
same pattern. McGee ran toward the Kansas City
cornerback, then cut toward the goal posts. Starr
lined a pass that shot underneath the crossbar,
hitting McGee in the hands and popping up into
the air. McGee turned and grabbed the ball out
of the air, all alone in the end zone. The Packers
led, 28-10.

A little later the Chiefs' Willie Mitchell intercepted a long Bart Starr pass. But when Lenny
Dawson couldn't get the Chiefs moving, they
punted the ball back to the Packers.

In came Starr again, the ball on his own
twenty. "You can bet he won't pass now," said a
Chief fan. "He's still thinking about that interception."

Starr threw another pass — right into the area
covered by Willie Mitchell. Carroll Dale caught
the pass for a twenty-five-yard gain.

Moments later Starr threw again, a pass into
Mitchell's zone. Max McGee grabbed the pass
and now the ball sat on the Chiefs' seventeen-
yard line. Five plays later Elijah Pitts swept into
the end zone for another Packer touchdown.
Green Bay led, 35-10.

At this point a merciful Lombardi took Starr
out of the game. And seven minutes later a gun-

shot ended the misery for the Chiefs, who walked off 35-10 losers. "The Packers are great," said a writer high in the press box. "But that Bart Starr, he's super-great."

Most of the other writers agreed. In the steamy Green Bay clubhouse, Al Silverman, the editor of *Sport Magazine,* pushed through the throng around Starr's locker.

"You win the sports car, Bart," said Al Silverman. "*Sport Magazine* has picked you as the Most Valuable Player in the Super Bowl. Here are the keys to a brand new 1967 Corvette."

"Thank you, sir," said Starr, who calls most everyone sir. "This is real kind of you. I guess I'll sound corny when I say it, but I think the credit should go to my blockers and my receivers."

Al Silverman, all the writers, and all the players and coaches, had no doubt who should get the Corvette: Bart Starr.

And a look at the statistics of the game told why: In this tense game of games, the players fighting to win $15,000 a man, Starr had thrown twenty-three passes and completed sixteen of them. All told he'd gained 250 yards with his passes, and two of those passes ended up in the end zone for touchdowns.

Those statistics didn't tell the full story of how great Bart Starr had been on this warm afternoon. Seven times he dropped back to pass on third down, knowing he had to complete the pass or give the Chiefs the ball. Five times he completed the pass.

What happened the other two times? Well, once a tackler knocked him down before he could release the pass. The other time the receiver dropped the ball.

In the Chiefs' clubhouse, coach Hank Stram shook his round head and said: "The thing that kept Green Bay going all day was Starr's ability — it was uncanny — to come up with the successful third-down play. Starr was the biggest single difference between the two teams."

Big defensive end Chuck Hurston came by. "I've never seen anything like it," said Hurston. "Once I was this close to him." Hurston held his fingers an inch apart. "Still he threw a touchdown pass. He's so calm. He didn't even notice me."

Tackle Jerry Mays nodded. "He is the most accurate passer I've ever seen," he said. "And nothing ever seems to upset his cool."

In the Packer dressing room, a reporter stopped Starr as he was walking calmly to the showers. "You were only a fair passer a few years ago," said the reporter. "How come you are so great today?"

Starr looked at the man. "I'm sorry, sir," he said. "But I don't understand your question. Could you put it a different way?"

"Well," said the man. "Do you think you are a better passer today than you were a few years ago?"

"Oh, yes," said Starr in his calm, precise way. "I think I threw the ball about as well my first couple of seasons as a pro as I do today . . . For me, being a better passer has just been a part of the whole gradual process of maturing. . . ."

Then, amid the yells of a victor's dressing room, Bart the Cool walked to the showers.

2

What Bart Starr Is Really Like

THIS IS WHAT BART
Starr is like:

A burly Chicago Bear lineman rushes at him,
fists high, and an elbow smashes into Starr's face.
Starr crumples to the ground, blood gushing
from a split lip. The Bear looms over the fallen
Starr, grinning down at him. Then Starr snaps
something, hard words, and the Bear player
quickly turns and backs off.

Starr gets to his feet. He calls a play in the
huddle. He takes the snap from center, drops
into the pocket, and throws a touchdown pass
to Boyd Dowler. The Packers go on to beat the
Bears, 24-0, in this 1961 game and go on to win
their first National Football League championship.

Bart still remembers that game. "The big
thing," he once told me, "is that I didn't get so
mad at George that I lost my composure. That's
very important. The worst thing that can happen
to a quarterback is that he gets so mad he forgets
that hard knocks are part of the game. You get
all riled up, you are concerned with retaliation,

then your concentration on your game plan isn't there.

"The game of football, after all, is just like the game of life except that it's played in a shorter time period. In football, as in life, you have got to learn to overcome things like anger. And when you do overcome them, you are a better football player and a better man."

This is what Bart Starr is like:

It is the night before a big game against the Packers' long-time rivals, the Baltimore Colts. In their hotel rooms in Baltimore, the Packers watch television, play cards, or relax on their beds. Someone knocks on the door of the room shared by Bart Starr and defensive tackle Henry Jordan. Starr opens the door and says in his pleasant way, "Come on in."

Bart has a fair face, with wide cheekbones. The face narrows as it curves down to the chin, giving him a small mouth. His eyes are narrow and alert, his hair brown and wavy. Nearly always he looks as if he is wearing a new suit — crisp, pressed, and neatly groomed.

"Henry," Starr is saying to his roommate, "do you think I can stand wearing this shirt tonight? I wore it on the plane today, and it is a little wrinkled."

The balding, good-humored Jordan booms out a big laugh. "Wear the shirt," he says. "I want to see you looking grubby for once in your life. I'd enjoy seeing you without a shave and wearing a wrinkled shirt. Do it for me."

Smiling, Starr slips on the slightly wrinkled shirt but his face is clean-shaven. He goes out to dinner with Jordan and fullback Jim Taylor. After dinner he returns to his room. On a table is a notebook. It is filled with the plays he will call tomorrow against the Colts.

Starr looks at the notebook, but only for a quick review. He has all those plays frozen in his mind after a week of intensive practice.

Starr puts down the notebook. He picks up another book. It is the Bible, and he reads the Psalms for a while before he clicks off the lamp at the side of his bed and goes to sleep. He feels nervous about tomorrow's game, but he knows he is ready for it.

This, too, is what Bart Starr is like:

Early in the 1961 season, Starr ripped a muscle in his abdomen during practice. He couldn't straighten up and walk erect, but he said nothing. "I didn't want to tell Coach Lombardi about it," he said later. "He has enough problems. At first Novocaine shots helped, but then it got worse."

For six painful weeks it got worse. In several games Starr had to pass from a crouch. He couldn't straighten to throw.

During those six weeks, the Packers played six games. They won five of them, won them with Starr passing and running and calling plays — in pain.

Finally the Packers got a ten-day rest. During the rest Starr's abdomen healed. When Starr could walk straight again, someone told him how courageous he had been. "Oh, no," he said, with an embarrassed smile. "Coach Lombardi tells us that we got to keep playing with the small hurts."

Opposing coaches know what Bart Starr is like:

"Bart Starr is a great field general, maybe the greatest one there ever was," a coach like Allie Sherman of the Giants will tell you. "He has that rare ability to look at a defense and 'read' how it is set up against him."

There was a game against the Cleveland Browns in 1964. In the fourth period the Packers trailed, 14-7. Green Bay had the ball on its own forty-four-yard line, fourth down and inches to go. Would they go for the first down or punt?

With time running out, Starr looked to Lombardi on the sideline. Lombardi waved his thick fist. *Go for it!*

Now Starr had to pick the play. He stuck his head into the huddle, calling the play. As Bart's voice barked out instructions, the Packers stared at him, surprised. Then they clapped hands and burst from the huddle.

"I didn't have anything to do with that call," receiver Max McGee said later. "No thanks. I kind of shuddered in the huddle."

The Browns knew what was coming. A power play with Jim Taylor thrusting up the middle. The Packers came up to the line of scrimmage and set their line tight for a power play. The Browns dug in, tensing to repulse the charge of the Packers.

Starr took the snap as the two lines slammed into each other. Taylor barged by Starr and Starr stuck the football into the big fullback's abdomen. *Wham!* Taylor smacked into the line, but the big Cleveland linemen hurled him back. Then the linemen saw that Taylor didn't have the ball.

Bart Starr had the ball. He had pushed it into Taylor's abdomen, then pulled it back. Now he was darting back, looking downfield. Out there was Max McGee, left all alone by the Cleveland secondary, which had rushed by him to throw back Taylor. Calmly, Starr flipped a pass to

McGee, who ran some fifty yards to the Cleveland one. Moments later Taylor smashed into the line, this time carrying the ball. The score was tied, 14-14.

A few minutes later Bart steered the big Packer machine to the Cleveland four-yard line. There the Cleveland coach, Blanton Collier, hurried in several big men to make a goal-line stand.

Starr, hands on hips, watched the big Browns lumber onto the field. Then he ducked into the huddle and called the play. He took the snap and faked a handoff to Taylor, who ran into the line. The big Browns threw back the fullback while Starr, carrying the ball, ran around end, easily outrunning the big linemen, to score another Packer touchdown.

The Packers won the game, 28-21. "We made mistakes," said Collier in the loser's clubhouse. "And Starr capitalized on every mistake we made. There isn't any quarterback in this league who's smarter on his feet."

Even among other quarterbacks, there is awe in their voices when they talk about how Starr calls "automatics." To a quarterback, an automatic is a play called outside the huddle.

Often a quarterback will come up to the line of scrimmage and see that a defense has changed. Suddenly he realizes that the play he called in the huddle won't work against this defense. So he changes the play at the line of scrimmage by calling an automatic.

No one calls automatics faster or surer than Starr. "You never know when he's calling an automatic," says Washington linebacker Sam Huff. "Some of the quarterbacks take a long time about it. But not Starr. He thinks fast."

Starr calls an automatic by quickening or slowing down the speed of his words as he barks out the signals. If he speaks fast, that may mean a pass. If he speaks slowly, that may mean a run.

He must call the automatic in a clear, concise voice, so that each Packer hears him. And he must call it amid the tension of a game, a third-and-one situation, the crowd roaring, big linemen glaring down his throat.

Vince Lombardi knows what Bart Starr is like:

"By the nature of his position your quarterback is your No. One man," he once wrote in a book, *Run to Daylight*. "I know that Bart feels he has the burden of our offense on his shoulders. As a result, I must try to relax him before each game. It's not that he lacks confidence. He has clearly developed that. It's just that, when you combine sincerity with sensitivity and intelligence, the individual tends to be tense."

"I'll say I'm tense," said Starr. "I'm nervous before every game. I can't even recall a scrimmage that didn't make me nervous."

At one time he would be so nervous he didn't have the confidence every pro quarterback must have to boss a team. Then Lombardi came to Green Bay and he drilled confidence into Starr.

One day recently Starr walked into Lombardi's office. He dropped a contract onto his coach's desk. "I didn't sign it," he told Lombardi. "There are some things in there I don't like."

Lombardi stared at him, this young man who had once been so shy. "A couple of years ago," said Starr, "I'd have signed anything you gave me. But now that you've taught me to be more aggressive and self-assertive, this is what I want."

And Starr told Lombardi exactly how much money he wanted.

The coach looked at his quarterback from behind his rimmed metal glasses. Then he barked a loud, raspy laugh. "So that's it," said Lombardi. "Like Frankenstein, I've created a monster."

The Packers know what Bart Starr is really like:

In a game several years ago against the Detroit Lions, the big Detroit linemen blew down Starr's blockers. On play after play, 300-pound Roger Brown or 275-pound Alex Karras slammed into Starr, sending him reeling to the grass. Starr got up after each knockdown, face grim, but silent. Not once did he blame his blockers.

"No one feels worse about it when they miss a block than the blockers do," Starr said later. "When Fuzzy Thurston [a Green Bay lineman] misses Roger Brown over and over again, there's no one in the stadium who feels worse than Fuzzy. So why yell at him? He knows it. Anyway, I've had great pass protection and yet thrown an interception. When that happened the blockers didn't blast *me*. So why should I blast *them* when they miss one?"

After that Detroit game a bruised Starr slumped on a stool in the clubhouse. From the other side of the room, Packer center Jim Ringo looked at his quarterback. "Bart should have been voted the most courageous athlete of the year for coming out in the second half," said Ringo. "But he never complained once. Not a word."

Ringo paused a moment. "But I'll tell you," he said. "Sometimes it's better if the quarterback is quiet. It makes a blocker feel bad when he's missed his block and he sees what happened to Bart."

His Packer teammates remembered what Detroit had done to Bart. The next time Green Bay played Detroit, the Packers won, 9-7. And only once in that game did a Lion lineman put a hand on Bart Starr. Whenever the Lions blitzed, the Packer blockers bounced them back.

"He's not emotional during a game," guard Jerry Kramer once said. "He doesn't get excited. I remember when we were trying to pick up momentum in a game, he yelled at me: 'C'mon Jerry, let's go!' The next day he apologized to me for saying it. I guess he thought he had made me feel bad in front of the team."

The teen-agers in Green Bay know what Starr is really like:

Starr lives with his wife and two young sons in a house a half-mile from where the Packers play. From his front door Bart can see the stadium where he plays. In the off-season Bart endorses various products as a sales-promotion man for different companies. When he leaves pro football, he has a $100,000-a-year offer to be a salesman for a Milwaukee stock brokerage firm.

Much of his off-season time is spent giving talks to groups of boys, including the Boy Scouts. Bart gives the boys tips on football — and on other things as well. Bart doesn't drink or smoke. He tells boys: "A lot of people think you are a sissy if you don't smoke or drink. Well, I know a lot of pro football players who don't smoke or drink — people like Fran Tarkenton and Bill Glass. I don't think you would call Fran Tarkenton or Bill Glass a sissy."

His opponents know what Starr is really like:

"He's quiet, too quiet," says Sam Huff. "Defensive guys like myself, we like to get a quarterback all excited and mad. Bart doesn't give you any satisfaction at all. In all my years of tackling him, I've never heard him complain."

The record books know what Bart Starr is really like:

In 1966 he completed 62 per cent of his passes — the best percentage in pro football. Over his career he has completed 57 per cent of his passes, the highest percentage of any NFL quarterback. During one stretch of time, through games over much of two seasons, Bart Starr threw 294 consecutive passes without having one intercepted — and that's an NFL record. He has had fewer pass interceptions than any other NFL quarterback — fewer than one every twenty-three times he's gone back to pass.

This, then, is what Bart Starr is really like. He is poised, friendly, easy going, relaxed. He is quietly confident. He is a quick thinker, an on-target passer, a methodical wrecker of defenses.

He is all of those things. But when you know about Bryan Bartlett Starr, you still don't know what Bart Starr is really like.

To know him, you have to know what it is like to be a high school quarterback nobody thinks will ever be great. You have to know what it's like to be a college star forced to sit on the bench.

You have to know what it's like to be a pro quarterback walking the streets in despair after being ignored by your coach. You have to know what it is like to brood all night long, sleepless, after throwing three intercepted passes that cost your team a victory.

And you have to know the joy of suddenly becoming a champion after years of bitterness, frustration, and disappointment. You have to know what it is like to be the quarterback nobody wanted, then to be saluted as the Most Valuable Player in the National Football League, and then the Most Valuable Player in pro football's first Super Bowl.

All this has happened to Bryan Bartlett Starr. To know what he is really like, you have to know how those things happened to him, and what those things did to him.

3

High School Quarterback

"HUP . . . HUP . . . hup. Left, right, left. . . ."

The drill sergeant's chant floated over the sun-baked drill field. Behind him the platoon of soldiers marched smartly, rifles angled on their shoulders. The time was 1942, a time of war. Here, at this Alabama Air Corps base, sergeants were training raw recruits to fight the Nazis and the Japanese.

One of those sergeants was Benjamin Bryan Starr, a hulking three-striper. In high school he had been a big pass-catching end. He had also boxed in high school, and his boxer's muscles rippled under his tight-fitting army jacket. He had just stepped out of his house, near the Maxwell Air Field, when he saw his eight-year-old son, Bart, on the front lawn. In Bart's hand was a football.

"I've got some time this afternoon," his father told Bart. "Let's play a little football."

"Touch or tackle football?" asked Bart.

"Well," said Bart's father, "you can tackle me and I'll tag you."

"O.K.," said Bart. "You kick off to me."

His father booted the ball to Bart, who caught it on the fly. He ran up the lawn, twisting to evade his father's tag.

"Got you!" said his father, tagging Bart.

Other boys soon joined the game. His father gave the boys tips on how to throw the ball, how to catch it, and how to make up plays. Years later Bart said that his father was his first football coach.

Sometimes, when Bart threw the ball, it fluttered to the ground like a sick bird. "My hands are too small," said Bart, staring in disgust at his fingers.

"Your hands will get bigger," said his father. "Even though you're having trouble throwing that big ball, keep practicing with it. Don't get too accustomed to throwing a smaller ball. If you do, you'll have trouble throwing a regulation-size ball when you're older."

For Bart and his father, football was for the fall and winter. In the spring his father hit long flies to Bart in the outfield, and in the summer Bart sometimes played with his father and other sergeants in baseball games.

The Starrs moved to Air Force posts in Florida and California. On those posts, amid the bugle calls and the tramp-tramp-tramp of combat boots, young Bart went to school with other children of Air Force men. After school he played every kind of sport — running races, hitting baseballs, shooting basketballs, kicking footballs. In the evenings, off-duty, Sgt. Starr pitched baseballs to Bart, or they ran foot races. And in the autumn they tossed a football to each other until it was too dark to see the ball.

Bryan Bartlett Starr was born in Montgomery,

Alabama, on January 9, 1934. Bryan was his father's middle name. Bartlett was the name of
his mother's doctor, a close family friend. For
a while his parents called him Bryan, but pretty
soon they called him Bart, a name that stuck.

When Bart was junior high school age, his fa-
ther was assigned to Maxwell Air Field near
Montgomery. Bart went to Baldwin Junior High
School. Baldwin boasted a fine football team.
Bart tried out for the team and, at first, didn't
impress anyone.

He wasn't fast, he wasn't big. But whenever
he took the ball, Bart somehow broke through
the line for ten- and twenty-yard gains. "You
look at him," said his coach, "and you hardly notice him. I mean, there's nothing stand-out about
him. Then the game begins and he's running
through the line for big gains."

In the spring of 1949, fifteen-year-old Bart trotted out for spring football practice at Sidney
Lanier High School. The Lanier head coach, Bill
Mosely, was a stern and unsmiling man. He de-
manded that every boy under him do what he
was told or get off the squad.

At first Mosely's eyes looked at Bart only
briefly. "Bart had no particularly outstanding
natural athletic ability or 'hot' talent," Mosely remembers. "Starr wasn't a big kid either. He
wasn't one of those strong, rawhide-tough kids.
And there wasn't anything real special about the
way he threw the ball. There wasn't anything
that might have caused us to pay particular attention to his passing that spring.

"But I'll tell you something about him. Bart
was alert and he was a good listener. He was as

attentive as you ever find in high school boys out for sports.

"He didn't mess around as some fellows do. Strictly business. Always listening, taking in every word we'd say. You knew he was out there to play football — to make the team."

For most of his first football season at Lanier, Bart sat on the bench. Lanier played the best teams in the state, each game a rugged struggle. Only late in the game, the battle won or lost, did Starr come running onto the field to replace Lanier's No. One quarterback.

In practice Starr threw and threw to put more zip on his passes. With his small hands he couldn't grip the ball across the laces. Sometimes his spirals wobbled drunkenly.

"You'll never be a passer," some of his pals told him.

Starr kept on throwing. He didn't say so, but deep inside Bart Starr there was the belief that if you worked hard enough to do something, you would do it. Starr saw a lot of boys who could pass better than he could. But they didn't stay on the gridiron for hours, throwing footballs to spots on the field, long after everyone else had gone. All that throwing, holding the ball near the nose, made Starr as good a passer as boys with bigger hands. Soon all that throwing made him a better passer than boys who had more talent — but who wouldn't work to polish the talent.

At the start of the 1950 football season, now a junior, Bart ranked as Lanier's No. Two quarterback. In the first game of the season, the No. One quarterback broke a leg. "Starr," said Coach Mosely, "get in there."

Starr ran out onto the field, nervousness making his stomach seem to melt. But after the first few plays, the nervousness vanished and Bart was calling plays with crisp confidence. Suddenly, as the pro football players say, "it all came together" for Starr. Everything he had learned, and practiced, on the football field suddenly jelled inside him. Just like that, he was an accomplished high school quarterback.

Mosely still can't get over how quickly it all happened. "He stepped in there," he says, "and played seven ball games like you've never seen a boy play."

Led by Starr, Lanier defeated the best teams in the state: Tuscaloosa, Selma, Dothan. Big crowds came out to see him, and in the crowd, of course, were Sgt. and Mrs. Ben Starr.

Watching from the stands, they saw Bart fade back. "He's going to pass," yelled Mr. Starr. He and his wife stood up with everyone else, looking downfield as Bart threw a long arching spiral.

"He's got it! He's got it!" yelled Bart's dad as a Lanier end raced under the falling ball. The Lanier end grabbed the ball and toppled into the end zone. Another touchdown for Lanier! And from the stands, Bart's first coach — his dad — joined in the applause as Bart and the receiver trotted off.

For Bart, though, quarterbacking wasn't all in hearing the cheers. There was hard, grinding work, day after day. During the week Coach Mosely and Bart often met in a corner of the locker room. "Look at this," said the coach one day, showing Bart thick sheets of papers. They were new plays.

Within a couple of weeks Bart had mastered the plays. He knew where he was supposed to run on each play, and he knew where each of his ten teammates was supposed to be.

"Bart," says Mosely, "was the kind of high school player we coaches would sit down with and map an entire new series of offensive plays. It was special stuff we built around Bart, diagrammed to take advantage of his particular capabilities. That's how good he was at Lanier. Bart Starr was the finest high school passer I've ever watched throw a football."

On some of those plays, Starr took the ball and ran, left or right, a few yards behind the line of scrimmage. This was Mosely's option play.

"Pass! Pass!" the defense yelled the first time Starr tried the option. The defense faded back to cover receivers.

Starr cocked the ball in his right hand, waving it as though he were about to throw. Then, suddenly, he burst through a hole in the line, snaking his way twenty yards downfield through the thinned-out defense.

"Bart learned all those new plays quickly," remembers Mosely. "He could soak up instruction the way a sponge takes water. You explained a play just once, and right away he'd run through it perfectly."

In Bart's senior year, 1951, the team went north to play one of Kentucky's fiercest teams, Louisville's Manual High. College scouts from all over the country were in the stands. Watching with binoculars, they wanted to see if this young Starr, talked about so much in Alabama, would fold up against the battering-ram pass rush of Manual.

Early in the game Bart stepped back to pass. In came a wave of tacklers, arms stretched high. Bart slipped out of one lineman's grasp, as elusive as a worm. He ran toward the sideline, the big and fast linemen straining at his heels. Bart seemed to be ignoring them, looking downfield for his receivers.

A lineman grabbed his shoulder. Bart gave a quick twist of his hips, and the lineman flew by him. Another rushed him, Bart ducked, and the tackler flew over Bart's shoulder. Then, as calm as a man pitching horseshoes, Bart Starr stood up and threw a pass to a receiver all alone twenty yards downfield.

And up in the stands the coaches knew how this boy from Alabama would stand up against a pass rush.

Slowly, carefully, and thoughtfully, Starr maneuvered the Lanier team downfield against the heavier Manual team. Lanier pushed across for one touchdown, then another. And up in the stands the college coaches shook their heads. One said to another: "I've got to get that boy for my school."

"Well, I don't know," said the other. "If you get him for your school, you're going to have to beat me out. I want him for my school."

And then the two scouts scampered down the stairs to talk to Starr in the locker room.

Dozens of scouts came by to talk to Starr. He could go to colleges in California, New England. Would he like to study a lot of easy courses on a sunny Florida campus? Would he like to play for a Big Ten school and become a famous All-American?

A year earlier Bart had played football on

the University of Kentucky campus, invited
there by then-coach "Bear" Bryant. Bryant had
shown him the Kentucky offensive system. Then
Bryant had introduced him to Babe Parilli: Kentucky Babe Parilli — All-American quarterback
at Kentucky — Bart Starr's idol.

Bart's eyes shined as he shook the great Babe's
hand. Then he and the great Babe walked out
onto the practice field. He was standing next to
the college quarterback he'd watched from the
stands, whom he had applauded. Now that quarterback, his idol, was talking to him, giving him
tips on how to play quarterback.

When the day ended, Bart was sure he would
enroll at Kentucky. Then something happened.

4

Then Came the Miseries

ALABAMA? OR KEN-
tucky? When someone asked him that question
in his senior year at high school, Bart said: "Oh,
I'm pretty sure I'm going up to Kentucky to play
for Mr. Bryant."

He had liked the rolling green campus of Kentucky. He had liked Bear Bryant. And he had
come away still excited, inside himself, after
meeting and talking with his idol, Babe Parilli.

"Babe," Starr said, "is the kind of quarterback
I hope I will be someday."

Someday, Bart hoped, high school kids would
talk about Bart Starr in the respectful way he
talked about Babe Parilli. What better way to follow Babe's footsteps than to succeed Babe as the
University of Kentucky's No. One quarterback?

He did think about the University of Alabama. Raised most of his life on Alabama soil,
Bart knew of the Crimson Tide and its proud
teams down through the years — the Rose Bowl
teams of 1926 and 1927, the Sugar Bowl teams
of 1945 and 1948, the Orange Bowl team of
1943, the Cotton Bowl team of 1942.

It was an honor, Bart knew, to be invited to

play for the Crimson Tide. But at Kentucky
there was Bear Bryant — and the legend of Babe
Parilli, the Kentucky Babe, Bart's idol.

A few days before he was going to be grad-
uated from Lanier, Bart was ready to sign a pa-
per promising to go to Kentucky. But then he
started to do some thinking.

His high school sweetheart, Cherry Morton,
said she was going to Auburn, an Alabama
school. "Gee," said Bart, "if I go to Kentucky I'm
going to be a long way from Cherry. An awful
long way." Cherry might meet another boy while
Bart was so far away. Bart thought about that a
little longer. Then he signed to go to the University of Alabama.

The Alabama coach, Red Drew, clapped his
hands with delight when he heard the great Lanier quarterback, Bart Starr, would wear the uni-
form of the Crimson Tide. The time was the fall
of 1952. Across the Pacific the guns of war
boomed in Korea. With many young men
drafted out of football jerseys and into khaki, the
Southeastern Conference — of which Alabama
was a member — allowed freshmen to play varsity football.

Only a few freshmen, though, made the starting lineups of the football teams. This was the
Southeastern Conference, a tough league filled
with some of the nation's powerhouse elevens:
Auburn, Alabama, Kentucky, Mississippi, and
Tennessee. In that freshman year of 1952, Starr
played enough minutes to earn a varsity letter.

That season Alabama went to the Orange
Bowl on New Year's Day to play Syracuse. The
Crimson Tide rolled over Syracuse, winning 61-6.
Late in the game Starr came in to run the team.

He threw twelve passes, completing eight of them, moving the Tide ninety-three yards. And one of his passes was caught in the end zone for a touchdown.

Touchdown! As the referee's arms shot high into the air, the Alabama rooters let out another happy roar. Bart Starr turned and ran off the field, head down, calm and poised. "Look at him," said an Alabama rooter. "He's only a freshman, he's just thrown a touchdown pass in the Orange Bowl, and look how cool he is."

In 1953, Bart's sophomore season, he started the season as Alabama's No. One quarterback. At the end of that season, Alabama coaches were insisting that Bart Starr was the best passer in the history of Alabama, greater even than the Crimson Tide's legendary Harry Gilmer.

In his best year Harry Gilmer had thrown for 930 yards. Bart Starr missed one game, but the soph completed 59 out of 119 passes for 870 yards. He threw eight of those passes for touchdowns — the most thrown by any passer in the Southeastern Conference.

He showed two qualities that year, qualities which would one day make him a great pro passer. One: His amazing bull's-eye accuracy on short and medium-range passes. Second: An uncanny ability to throw passes without being intercepted. In that 1953 season, only six of Bart's 119 passes were picked off by the enemy, an astonishing percentage for a college passer.

That season Bart also did the punting for the Crimson Tide. His average, 41 yards a kick, was second best in the nation. But one day the next summer, one punt would cripple Bart Starr and begin a long and dreary six years filled, for the most part, with gloom and misery and bitter disappointments.

In August 1954, Bart Starr was twenty years old. For most of those twenty years he had known only success — blinding, brilliant success. He had been a sensational high school quarterback, a crack baseball and basketball player in high school. In classrooms he learned quickly and easily. He had accepted success with a cool poise. He never bragged. He never exulted over a defeated opponent.

Now he would know six years of failure, the ashen taste of defeat nearly always in his mouth. He would learn what it is like to be a loser on a team of losers.

Bart Starr did not accept being a loser. It hurt him like the sting of a dentist's drill on the nerve endings. He was unhappy. Sometimes he wondered if he weren't chasing after something he could never catch, like a small boy trying to catch the wind.

But through all the losing, Bart Starr was never the sore loser. He never whined to teammates that he wasn't getting a chance. He never sulked in practice. He never threw up his hands and said, "I quit."

In defeat, at least on the surface, he was the poised gentleman. Inside he burned, raging to prove himself. But rarely did he let that rage shatter his poise.

And one day a coach — his name was Vince Lombardi — noticed how Bart Starr behaved in defeat. Lombardi liked what he saw. It led to a decision that would turn years of losing into years of winning — for Bart Starr and for the Green Bay Packers.

On this August day in 1954, working out on the practice field at the University of Alabama, Bart boomed a long kick downfield. He watched the kick spiral toward the ground. He shook his head.

"That was beautiful," said a player with him.

"No," said Bart, a perfectionist. "It wobbled a little. Somewhere I'm doing something wrong."

He picked up another ball, held it a moment, then dropped it. Up swung his right leg, the instep of the foot whamming into the ball. At impact Bart skipped off his left foot. When he did, something went *pop!* in Starr's back.

"I think maybe I hurt something," Starr said, holding his back.

He picked up another ball and kicked it. Now the back really began to hurt. He kicked another ball, but it wobbled off the side of his foot. "I'd better rest for awhile," said Starr. "I don't feel right."

He wouldn't feel right for a year.

The next day he tried to pass. He cocked his arm, threw, and the ball wobbled through the air and bounced on the grass, ten yards short of the receiver.

"Let me try again," he said, taking another snap from center.

Back he went. He lifted his right arm, and his back flared with pain. "After awhile," he told me recently, "I finally got to the point where I couldn't do anything."

He limped off to a hospital. Doctors put him in bed and X-rayed the back. "It looks," said the doctors, "like your sacroiliac has slipped out."

The doctors explained to Starr that the sacroiliac, a joint in the base of the back, is part of the spine. If the sacroiliac slips, sensitive nerves flash pain through the body.

"You don't have to tell me," said Starr. "I feel the pain."

Despite the pain Starr hobbled out of the hospital and tried to work out with the rest of the team. Pain riddled his back and Starr trudged back to the hospital.

He missed all of the preseason practice. When the season started, he tried to play, but now the pain was so bad Starr could barely lift his right arm above the shoulder.

"I was in and out of the hospital so much that season," says Starr now, "that I was messed up for the entire season."

In that 1954 season, getting to play only in pain, Starr was still the bull's-eye accurate passer. He threw only 41 passes all season long, but he connected with 24 of them.

A year of rest took the pain out of his back. By the summer of 1955, the football season only a month away, Bart felt fit and ready to burst loose on the football field.

Then came a new problem.

At the end of the disappointing 1954 season, Red Drew resigned as Alabama's coach. He was replaced by J. B. (Ears) Whitworth.

When Whitworth arrived at the Alabama campus in the spring of 1954, he noticed something that made him wonder. "I have a feeling," he said to an assistant, "that some of these seniors have grown accustomed to losing. They had a losing team last year, and maybe they think they're going to have a losing team this year. That isn't a good attitude."

Whitworth was so unhappy with his seniors

that when the season began, he started a team of sophs and juniors. The seniors sat on the bench.

Bart Starr was stunned at being left on the bench. He had been the starting quarterback as a sophomore. Now, a senior, he wasn't good enough to start.

Today he can talk about that year calmly. But the memory still smolders in his chest. "This will happen in many cases when a new coach comes in," he says. "He tries to build for the future. I guess he thought that some of the seniors who had been around there for awhile didn't have the best attitude in the world. So he decided to play the younger fellows."

Starr sat on the bench most of that year. He threw only 96 passes as a backup quarterback, but as always he was on-target better than fifty per cent of the time, completing 55.

Mostly he played when Alabama trailed hopelessly. With mostly sophs and juniors in the lineup, the once-proud Crimson Tide lost all ten games.

"It just killed me," says Starr. "When you're hurt and not playing, like I was in my junior year, naturally it's depressing. But when you're *not* hurt and you're *not* playing, when you sit on the bench while your team loses, naturally you think you could be doing better than the people who are out there.

"I was not a particularly tough person at that stage of my life. In fact, I was probably anything but. Probably any confidence that I had built up in twenty years of life was gone. A guy just sits there and doesn't play. Ridiculous."

When the coach did send Starr into a game, Bart wasn't the leader he had been two years ear-

lier. "I was — oh, withdrawn, and just plain de-
pressed over the entire situation," he says.
"When I'd go out there on the field, I'm sure I
wasn't the type of leader I should have been."

Starr played so little during his senior year
that no National Football League team looked
closely at him. When the draft meetings began,
each club in turn picking a college player, the
first round went by, then the second round, then
the third round. Not one club picked Starr.

The drafting went on all afternoon and late
into the evening. One hundred of the top college
players had been drafted. These players would
get a chance, the following summer, to try out
for a pro club. Now one hundred and fifty had
been drafted, then almost two hundred.

Now it was Green Bay's turn to pick its seven-
teenth draft choice. An assistant coach looked at
a typed list of the players who were still avail-
able.

"This Starr down at Alabama," said the coach.
"We don't have much information on him. But
he's supposed to be one of those Phi Beta Kap-
pas. If he's that smart, maybe he can learn."

The Packers drafted Starr.

Bart Starr was *not* a Phi Beta Kappa honor
student. "And with my confidence gone," he said
recently, "I wasn't the type of leader you have to
be to lead a professional club."

He had played hardly at all in his senior year.
His confidence was shattered. He had been
drafted only by accident — a fluke.

But Bart Starr wasn't giving up. And he was
determined to make the most of that accident,
that fluke.

5

Vince Needs a Quarterback

THE SEARING SUMMER sun hung, hot and frying, over the backyard in Macon, Mississippi. If you had hovered over that backyard in a helicopter, you would have stared down at a strange sight.

Down below you would have seen a tall, broad-shouldered young man in T-shirt and shorts. In his right hand he held a football. Some twenty yards away from him, hanging by a rope from the limb of a tree, swayed an automobile tire. Some fifteen yards behind the tire, sweat running down her face, stood a slender girl.

The young man threw the ball. It whistled through the tire, hitting the ground and bouncing up into the arms of the girl. Wearily, she threw the ball, in that awkward way that girls have, back to the young passer.

"O.K. Cherry," said the passer. "Now I'm going to try throwing the ball through the tire from this angle."

He walked about twenty paces to his left, aimed and fired the ball through the tire. The girl picked up the bouncing football and lofted it back to him.

Cherry and Bart Starr had been doing this all afternoon on this hot summer's day. All summer long, in fact, Bart had been throwing footballs at this tire, sharpening his passing eye so he would be ready when he reported to the Green Bay summer camp.

Starr wasn't making the mistake so many rookies make. "They come to camp," a New York Giant coach once told me, "thinking: 'I'm an All-American. I don't have to worry about making the team.' When they get to camp they find they are one of dozens of All-Americans. And the other All-Americans are in shape to play football. Right away they are behind everyone else. They can never catch up. It's a shame. They beat themselves before they ever get started."

Bart Starr knew he had some catching up to do. He was going to camp to battle for a job against quarterbacks who had played ten to twelve games the season before — as collegians or as pros. Starr had played only every once in awhile. He knew he was rusty. Now, before he went to camp, Bart wanted to scrape off that rust.

"I was lucky to be going to the Green Bay camp at all," Starr says now. "One reason I got there was because Johnny Dee was then the basketball coach at Alabama. Even though I hadn't played much my last two seasons at Alabama, he thought I could play pro ball.

"Johnny had a friend who was a Green Bay scout. He talked his friend into giving me that chance. If he hadn't done that, I guess I never would have played pro ball."

Then, too, the Green Bay coaches thought Starr was a Phi Beta Kappa. Another break. It was the kind of break that has happened to many pro quarterbacks. As a rookie Johnny Unitas was rejected by the Pittsburgh Steelers. Nearly penniless, he hitchhiked a ride home to Pittsburgh from the Steeler training camp. But then the Baltimore Colts spotted his name on a list of free-agent players. The Colts took a chance, hired him, and Unitas became a star.

A break. A bit of luck. And something else.

After the Steelers cut him, Unitas kept himself in shape, passing for a Pittsburgh semipro team. When the break came along, he was ready to take advantage of it.

Starr flew to the Green Bay camp that summer of 1956 figuring he would need any number of lucky breaks. After that terrible year on the bench at Alabama, he once said, "I was down as low as I have ever been. That was the year I started doubting my own ability."

When he arrived at the Green Bay camp, Starr saw the list of quarterbacks. The list was posted on the wall in one of the dormitories where the Packers lived and slept. What Starr saw would have sunk the stomach of even the most breezily confident of quarterbacks. Starr ranked fifth among the five quarterbacks in camp.

No. One quarterback was the easy going veteran Tobin Rote. Starr roomed with Rote. "He taught me a lot," Starr remembers. "He was a real hard-nosed guy. He had his own style and he was set in it. But he treated me just fine, and he gave me tips. He didn't have to do that. The first thing he told me was, 'Kid, you have to learn to zip the ball a little. You won't make it in this league throwing cream puffs.'

"He had tremendous courage, too. He took his

lumps and never said a word. That's something else I learned from him."

At camp Bart — and all the other rookies — lived in dread of The Turk. In every pro football camp, The Turk is the assistant coach who walks, late at night, the dormitory floors (most pro teams train at private prep schools). He comes on a grim errand from the head coach. The Turk knocks on the door of a player's room and says: "Coach wants to see you."

His heart sinking, the player knows what that invitation means. But then he thinks: "No, no, maybe I'm wrong. Maybe the coach just has a question he wants to ask me."

Fearfully the player dresses and goes with The Turk to the coach's room. He goes into the room alone. There, quietly and politely, he is told he has not made the team. He is being cut. The coach hopes he will catch on with some other pro team. Good-by and good luck, and please turn in your playbook before you leave.

Sometimes the player leaves that night, walking out into the darkness. If he waits until morning, he usually leaves at dawn, ashamed to face the other players.

In the morning the other players look at his empty bed and nod to each other: "The Turk has struck again." They don't smile, and no one even mentions the name of the player who is gone. Pro football players are a superstitious lot. If you mention the name of a player whom The Turk has visited, maybe the next night The Turk will visit you.

That summer The Turk walked often by the door of Bart Starr. On the night when the coaches were making their last cuts before the

start of the season, Starr went to bed nervous
and worried. As he stretched there, eyes wide
and staring at the ceiling, he looked back on the
training season. He hadn't done really well, but
he hadn't done badly.

He remembered one game against the Giants.
He'd taken over the team in the second half.
Back he went to pass, the Giant linemen flood-
ing in on him. He ducked away from one man,
then turned and completed the pass. Unruffled,
he completed another, then another. And down
on the Giant three-yard line, he had handed off
to his fullback, who plunged across the goal line.

Touchdown! Now, stretched on the bed, Starr
thought about that touchdown. He smiled.
Then, suddenly, the smile froze on his face.

Footsteps! Out in the hallway. Someone was
walking down the corridor toward his room.
Was it The Turk?

Starr thought he had stopped breathing. The
steps pounded closer to the door. Starr raised
himself on one elbow, hoping he wouldn't hear
that fateful knock — the knock that would end
his hopes of being a pro quarterback.

The steps were loud now, very loud. The Turk
was outside his door.

The Turk kept on walking, right past Starr's
door. "Until that final cut," said Starr later, "I
didn't know I had made the club. When I knew
I had, it was one of the happiest moments of
my life."

Head coach Lisle Blackbourn threw Starr into
games only occasionally during that 1956 season.
Bart trotted off the bench to replace Tobin Rote
usually when a game was hopelessly lost. He
threw only 44 passes, but as usual Bart com-

pleted well over fifty per cent of his passes, hitting receivers with 24 throws. And what Blackbourn liked especially was that only three of Bart's passes were intercepted.

Bart had remembered Tobin Rote's tip — he was zinging that ball through the air instead of cream puffing it. "You cream puff it in the NFL," Rote had told Starr, "and the defense will gather under it like outfielders under a pop fly."

Since 1946 the luckless Packers had not waged a winning season. The year 1956 was no exception. The Packers won four and lost eight — a record the booing Green Bay fans had come to dread.

In 1957 the Packers signed Paul Hornung, the Golden Boy, out of Notre Dame. As an Irish quarterback, Hornung had won the Heisman Trophy as the nation's best college player. But Hornung, a slashing runner, threw cream-puff passes. "He'll be a great pro runner," said Blackbourn. "But you can see he is no pro passer."

Desperate, Blackbourn traded away Tobin Rote for another quarterback — Babe Parilli. Suddenly Bart's old idol was now the Packers' No. One quarterback. And Bart, who had watched Kentucky Babe from the stands, was now battling him for that No. One job.

The Babe, though, was just as kind to Bart as he had been years before on the campus at the University of Kentucky. He showed Starr how he cupped his hands under the center to receive the snap, how he ran back into the pocket as fast as he could, and how he released the ball without any wasted motion. "In those early years," says Starr, "in high school and in my first three years with the pros, Babe taught me more about basic quarterback play than any coach."

The fabled Kentucky Babe, however, couldn't lift the Packers. In 1957 the Packers won only three games while losing nine. Green Bay fans howled for Blackbourn's resignation and the weary, unhappy coach quit.

Before leaving to coach at Marquette University Blackbourn talked with Starr. "You are going to have a tough time making it as a pro quarterback, Bart," said Blackbourn.

"I know," said Starr.

"Look," said the coach. "You have a quick way of understanding defenses. And you understand offenses. You've learned a lot here the past two years because you learn fast. I think you would be a good teacher of quarterbacks. Do you want to go to Marquette with me?"

"No, thanks," said Starr. "I'm going to try to make it as a pro quarterback."

Ray "Scooter" McLean succeeded Blackbourn. In 1958 the breezy McLean alternated Parilli and Starr at quarterback. "It was a kind of musical-chairs year," Starr remembers. "Babe played the most, though. When I got the chance, I just didn't do the job.

"It was discouraging for me to go home at the end of the season. I realized I had done so poorly. I wasn't mature enough emotionally to give leadership. I wasn't over that letdown I had in college.

"The only way to build confidence is to succeed. For three or four years now, I had not succeeded at anything in football — in college or with the Packers."

When Starr did not succeed — when he threw an interception — he seemed to come apart. "I lost confidence in my play calling, in my passing, in everything," he says. "I could not stand failure. I'd throw an interception and it'd kill me. I'd worry about it all during the game and this is bad."

Off the field Starr jumped when a coach criticized him for calling a certain play. "I was sensitive about criticism," he says. "I'm a sensitive person basically. At least my wife tells me I am."

Parilli couldn't move the Packers. And Starr, doubtful about himself and his passing, moved them into trouble. Not surprisingly, the Packers won only one game out of twelve in 1958. A horrified Packer management fired Ray McLean. The new coach: Vince Lombardi.

When Vince Lombardi played football for Fordham back in the 1930's, he stood on the Ram line as one of the legendary Seven Blocks of Granite. It was a line that threw back ball carriers as though they had barged into a stone wall. Twenty-five years later, after being an assistant coach at West Point and with the Giants, Lombardi still looked like a hunk of New Hampshire granite — a blocky body, a jaw like brick, and small eyes that glittered ferociously from behind steel-lined spectacles.

He also had a reputation for cracking the whip over his players. The Packers soon learned they must follow Lombardi's orders or be bounced off the club. Towering tackles cringed when he scolded them with his rasping, cutting voice. When he spoke at clubhouse meetings, beefy players dreaded scraping a chair on the floor and having to face those fierce glittering eyes.

Lombardi could be just as tough with the own-

ers of a ball club. "This is what I want," he
snapped when he came to Green Bay. The owners, anxious to get the Packers winning again,
made Lombardi general manager. He had the
power to make any trade he wanted to make.

Lombardi looked over the roster of players.
He talked to several of the Packers. Later, in
his book, *Run to Daylight*, Lombardi told of his
reaction to meeting Bart Starr.

"When I first met him," wrote Lombardi, "he
struck me as so polite and so self-effacing that I
wondered if maybe he wasn't too nice to be the
authoritarian leader that your quarterback must
be."

Then Lombardi looked at movies of the
1958 Packers. "I decided," he said, "the first
thing I needed was help at quarterback. So I
traded for Lamar McHan."

*The first thing I needed was help at quarter-
back.* A glum Starr read what Lombardi had
said. His confidence was now down to near
zero. "But I don't blame coach Lombardi for
trading for Lamar," Starr told a friend. "The
Packers do need a quarterback. I haven't been
doing the job. And now it looks like maybe I
never will."

6

Bart Starr — A Failure

LOMBARDI STARED, SURprise showing in his eyes. His three quarterbacks — Lamar McHan, Bart Starr, and Joe Francis — were sitting on stools around him in the bare room. From outside, through the thin walls, floated the shouts of the Packers, getting dressed in the clubhouse for their first preseason game of the 1959 season. Now, in this room, Lombardi listened as each of his three quarterbacks rattled off the game plan, the kind of plays they would call.

Starr had just finished speaking. He looked up at his coach. Lombardi couldn't keep the surprise out of his eyes. Later he explained why.

"Even though he was not first string," said Lombardi, "Bart repeated almost verbatim everything we had discussed the previous three days. That meant he had a great memory, dedication, and desire."

For a long while Lombardi remembered how dedicated and willing to work Starr had been — even when he wasn't playing. He liked that in a player, especially in a quarterback. That kind of player isn't likely to give up when he is down by three touchdowns. That kind, he knew, never gives up.

Consequently Lombardi kept Starr at Green Bay even while Bart was throwing interceptions and calling the wrong plays; in 1961 Lombardi would be happy he had kept Starr.

When he first met Starr, though, Lombardi wasn't impressed.

"When I joined the team," said the stocky coach, "the opinion around here and in the league was that Starr would never make it. They said he couldn't throw well enough and wasn't tough enough. They said he had no confidence in himself, and that no one on the team had any confidence in him. After looking at the movies the first preseason, I came to the conclusion that he did have the ability — the arm, the ball-handling techniques, and the intelligence. But what he needed was confidence."

At the Packers' summer camp in 1959, Starr's confidence, what little he had, was draining out of him. One afternoon he stepped back to pass and threw a ball five feet over the receiver's head, even though the receiver was only a little way downfield.

Starr kicked at the ground, angry at himself. He walked back into the huddle and called a play. Hovering over the huddle, listening, was the backfield coach.

"No, no," he growled. "You're calling that play to the wrong side, Starr. Don't you see that?"

Redfaced, his head down, Bart nodded. How long could he go on making mistakes like this? Yesterday he had read a newspaper story which claimed the Packers would release him before the season started. It could be that the newspaperman who had written the story had been talking to Lombardi. Maybe Lombardi had told the reporter he planned to have The Turk visit Starr's room.

"I felt like a rookie," Bart said later. "I'm sure I made mistakes as a four-year man that Lombardi wouldn't believe possible."

Starr looked around the huddle, the backfield coach listening to every word he would say. He called another play, this time to the correct side. "O.K.," yelled the coach. "Now you got it, Bart."

At the start of the season, Starr was still hanging on to the club, but McHan had won the job as No. One quarterback. Bart was No. Two, and Joe Francis was No. Three.

In their first game under coach Lombardi, the Packers astonished everyone in the National Football League. With Jim Taylor and Paul Hornung slicing up the middle and careening around the ends, the Packers upset the Monsters of the Midway, the Chicago Bears, 9-6.

Green Bay fans were smiling. They were laughing a week later when the Packers beat the Lions, 28-10. They were near delirious the following week when the Packers won their third straight, stopping the San Francisco 49ers in a thriller, 21-20.

The next Sunday the Los Angeles Rams came to play the Packers in Milwaukee (the Packers play some of their home games in Milwaukee, Wisconsin, and the rest in nearby Green Bay). In the streets of little Green Bay (population 62,888), people talked of the game with excitement shrilling their voices. Nothing in Green Bay is more important to the people than the

Packers, for the Packers are a Green Bay team — born and raised in this city on the shores of Lake Michigan.

On the evening of August 11, 1919, a group of broad-shouldered young men got together for a meeting in the newsroom of the Green Bay *Press Gazette*. Seated on chairs and desktops, they listened to hefty Curly Lambeau, who threw around crates for the Indian Packing Company during the day. A former college player, Curly wanted to start a semipro football team to play other teams for money.

"It's a great idea to have a team," someone said. "But who will pay for the uniforms? And where can we practice?"

Someone else said, "How about going to the Indian Packing Company? They might put up the money for the uniforms."

A little later the meeting broke up. The next day Curly talked to his bosses at the Indian Packing plant. "Sure," said one boss, "we'll pay for the team's jerseys, and you can use our athletic field for practice."

And so the Green Bay Packers were born. In 1920 the team won ten games and lost only one. In 1921 it joined the new National Football League, playing against teams like the Duluth Eskimos and the Frankford Yellow Jackets.

Like most professional football teams, the Packers lost money. Soon the Indian Packing Company said it could no longer afford to pay the bills. A group of Green Bay businessmen quickly huddled together, reached into their pockets, and came up with enough money to keep the team alive.

Today hundreds of Green Bay citizens — druggists, telephone clerks, salesmen — own shares in the Green Bay Packers. Some own $100 worth; others own $1,000, or $5,000. When Green Bay wins, they cheer. When Green Bay loses, each owner is sure he knows what went wrong. "They should have passed that time they had the ball on the twenty-yard line," they'll say. Or "Why didn't they send out Boyd Dowler on that long pass?"

During the season all the players live in Green Bay. When they walk down the streets, people walk right up to them and say: "Are we going to beat the Rams this week?"

"We're going to be out there trying," say the players. The fans slap them on the backs and say, "You go out there and get them, hear? And we'll be up there cheering for you all the way."

In the 1950's, though, the Packer fans had little to cheer about. The proud Packers, winners of NFL championships in the 1920's and '30's with such great stars as Don Hutson, Cecil Isbell, Johnny Blood, and Clark Hinkle, had not won an NFL championship since 1944. After winning only one game in 1958, it seemed the Packers might never win another NFL title.

The Packer owners, arguing among themselves, finally decided to hire Vince Lombardi as head coach. "I'm not a miracle man," Lombardi told them when he arrived in Green Bay. "But I'll do everything I can."

Now, on this Sunday afternoon in 1959, the owners had reason to think Lombardi was a miracle man. In the three weeks of this 1959 season, the Packers had won three games. Over the previous three seasons, they had won only a grand total of eight!

The fans, roaring for the Packers, filled Milwaukee's County Stadium for the game against the Rams. On the opening kickoff, the fans stood and cheered. For the rest of the game they sat quietly, faces grim, staring down at a disaster. The Rams slaughtered the Packers, 45-6.

"Same old team," grumbled some fans as they filed out of County Stadium. "Same old bunch of losers."

The next Sunday, with Lamar McHan passing accurately, the Packers scored three touchdowns against the Colts. But Johnny Unitas passed the ball through the Packer defense like water through a strainer. When the final score was flashed from Baltimore to Green Bay, the cold wind seemed even more frigid to the people of Green Bay. Their team had lost again, 38-21.

In that game McHan was injured. The No. Two quarterback, Bart Starr, hastily prepared himself for the next Sunday's game against the Giants in New York. "I thought this was going to be my big chance," Starr remembers. "I was loving it under Lombardi, learning from week to week."

The Packers flew into New York on a Saturday. On the plane Bart flipped through the pages of his playbook, noting the plays he planned to use against the Giants, deciding, as all pro quarterbacks do, what three or four plays he would use to open the game. "I had a real good game plan," he remembers.

Then Lombardi called a meeting of the quarterbacks. The three quarterbacks filed into the room — the injured Lamar McHan, his shoulder swathed in bandages; the tight-lipped Starr; the young Joe Francis.

Lombardi sat facing them. "All right," he said in his crisp, metallic voice. "You, Francis, are going to start."

Starr stared at Lombardi, surprise dropping open his jaw. He couldn't believe what he had heard. He was the No. Two quarterback. Why should Francis, the No. Three quarterback, get to start the game?

Always the obedient soldier, Starr said nothing. He tried to hide his shame and disappointment by looking down at his playbook. When the meeting ended, he jumped up and grabbed Francis by the shoulder. "Good luck, Joe," he said. "Go out there and knock them dead."

Francis grinned. Out he went onto the field at Yankee Stadium, leading the Packers. The big crowd of sixty thousand was shrieking, "Go-o-oh Giii-ants. Go-o-oh Giii-ants. . . ."

The Giants did go against the Packers, and Francis could not pick up the Packers and get them to go against the Giants. The Packers' offense, sputtering like a tin lizzy all afternoon, could not score a touchdown and the Giants won, 20-3.

Starr sat on the bench, fists clenched. He watched Francis move the Packers a few yards downfield. Then the drive would stop. He pounded fist against palm, anger flaring hot and red inside him. He could get this team moving. He was sure of it. But here he was, sitting on the bench, out of the action. Out of everything. He was a failure, a flop.

After the game Starr walked the streets for a long time. Maybe he didn't have the confidence a great quarterback needed. And maybe what they said was true — he didn't light the fire of inspiration inside his players. When he called a play, maybe the players figured: "This won't work because Starr himself doesn't believe it will work."

Bart Starr was a failure.

7

Victory!

"I'M A STARR MAN," snapped the Green Bay grocer.

"Well, I'm a McHan man," growled the milkman, anger in his voice. "Your man is terrible."

"Is that so?" said the grocer. The two men stared at each other, fists clenched, noses inches apart.

All over Green Bay, during 1959 and 1960, similar arguments raged. "It's like Republicans versus Democrats," said radio announcer Bob Houle. "You can divide this town into Starr men and McHan men."

The arguments first flared during the 1959 season when McHan was hurt. After that disaster in New York, Lombardi didn't dare to start young Joe Francis again.

The next Sunday Lombardi said to McHan: "Can you play?"

"I think I can," said McHan. His sore shoulder encased in padding, the grim-faced quarterback ran out onto the field. But near the end of the first period, he trotted off, biting his lip. "I'm sorry, coach," said McHan. "But I can't lift my arm to throw anymore."

Lombardi wheeled, his big jaw rapping out the order: "Bart Starr! Get on in there."

Starr ran in. A few plays later he pitched a touchdown pass. But the Bears won the game, 28-17.

The next Sunday Starr started against the Baltimore Colts. He and Johnny Unitas duelled brilliantly, the first of many contests they would have through the years, the Colts finally winning this one, 28-24. But even in defeat a lot of Green Bay fans stood and cheered Starr as he came off the field.

Bart started the next four games, the final four of the 1959 season. The Packers won the first three games. The last game of the season was against the San Francisco 49ers. During the week before that game, Bart could feel confidence — the confidence that had come so hard for him — growing inside himself.

"That was a real big game for me," he said after the San Francisco game. "I had studied coach's offense and how to read defenses. I knew, in theory, how to take advantage of what I knew.

"But it was still just theory. I had trouble seeing those things in a game. Against the 49ers, everything fell in place all at once. It was like lifting a veil in front of my eyes. I could look at the defense and see things I had never seen before."

Starr picked apart the 49ers' defense with his passes, winning 36-14. The victory gave the Packers a record of seven victories and five defeats — the team's first winning season in almost a decade. The Packers finished third in the Western Conference, a game behind the Bears, and only two games behind the champion Colts.

"That boy Starr is all right," Lombardi said after the 49er game. "We've got a couple of pretty good quarterbacks now — Lamar and Bart."

After steering the Packers to those final four victories of the 1959 season, Starr came to camp in the summer of 1960 figuring he now ranked ahead of McHan as the team's No. One quarterback. Again he ran smack into the stony wall of disappointment.

"I don't know who will be the No. One quarterback," Lombardi told McHan and Starr. "During the preseason games I'm going to alternate you. The one who moves the team, he is the one who gets the No. One job."

"Starting at quarterback . . . Bart Starr . . ." The announcer's voice boomed through City Stadium in Green Bay. In the preseason games, Bart had moved the Packers. Now he was starting in the Packers' opening game — against the Bears. On the sideline, Starr warmed up, flipping passes to Paul Hornung. He could feel the tension pinching his stomach. His hands were wet. He was opening the season as Green Bay's No. One quarterback. After all the gloomy years of disappointment, this was his chance to break out into the sunshine.

In the first period, he steered the Packers artfully down the field, mixing passes and runs, moving Green Bay to the Bears' thirty. But there, somehow, Starr couldn't pull off the magic play that would spring someone loose for a touchdown and the Bears threw back the Packers.

And so the game went. Starr moved the Packers into Bear territory, but only twice could he find the key to open the door of the end zone. Two touchdowns usually are not enough to win pro football games, and they were not enough this time. The Bears ran off the happy 17-14 winners. From the stands the McHan men booed Starr.

McHan started the next game for the Packers. He, too, couldn't pluck from his bag of plays the one play that would free somebody for a touchdown. Early in the game, Lombardi sent in Bart Starr.

Suddenly, Starr had the key. The Packers scored, and then quickly scored again. Jim Taylor punched across the middle for a touchdown. Paul Hornung looped around end for another touchdown. Green Bay won, 28-9.

The next week McHan started against the world champion Baltimore Colts, but early in the game Lombardi switched to Starr. Again Starr and Unitas pitted their arms and their brains against each other in a tingling duel, and this time Starr came out the master, the Packers winning 35-21.

After that game, Lombardi called Bart into his office. "Bart," said the coach. "You're it. You're No. One. Don't worry about a thing."

Lombardi had reason to talk that way to Starr. He had decided that Starr would be his No. One quarterback. He had seen how Starr's confidence had soared in the past year, and he wanted that confidence to stay high. When he told Starr, "Don't worry about a thing," he meant, "Don't doubt yourself."

Lombardi knew, though, that Starr would worry as long as McHan was behind him. Lombardi had an idea, but the idea would have to wait until after the end of the season.

Green Bay led the Western Conference with a 4-1 record. In second place were the Baltimore Colts with a 4-2 record. "They're coming to play us in Baltimore next Sunday," said Colt fullback Alan Ameche. "We'll show them that game they won in Green Bay was a fluke. We'll show them what we can do."

The Colts and Ameche quickly showed the Packers what they could do, running up a 21-0 lead. From the stands the Colt fans jeered at the Packers, yelling, "Good-by, Green Bay, good-by, Bart Starr. . . ." But Bart Starr was saying no good-bys. He began to throw, first to fullback Jim Taylor, then to end Boyd Dowler. Starr threw into the end zone for one touchdown. Paul Hornung swept around end for another.

A little later Hornung kicked a field goal. Starr threw another touchdown pass and suddenly, midway through the third period, the Packers had stormed back to tie the game, 24-24.

Wise old John Unitas, though, had seen something. One of the Packer safeties, Jesse Whittenton, had limped off the field, his ankle twisted. The Packers rushed in a rookie to replace Whittenton.

Looking out of his huddle, Unitas saw the rookie coming in. On the next play he shot his slickest receiver, Ray Berry, right at the rookie.

Whang! Unitas hit Berry with a pass. *Whang!* Unitas hit him again. He peppered the rookie's area with passes and within minutes the Colts led, 31-24.

The next time he had the ball, Unitas shot Berry once more at the rookie. *Whap!* Berry grabbed another pass. And another — this time taking the ball and dancing down the sideline like a man on a tightrope, racing into the end zone for another touchdown. Moments later the gun coughed, ending the game, the Colts 38-24 victors.

The Colts had been champions of the Western Conference for two straight years. In 1960 it looked like they were a cinch to win three straight.

With the season three-quarters done, the standings in the west looked like this:

	Won	Lost	Ties
BALTIMORE	6	3	0
CHICAGO	5	3	1
GREEN BAY	5	4	0

Most of the experts said the Colts would gallop away from the Bears and the Packers. "The Packers," wrote one sportswriter, "lack the balanced attack and the quarterback."

"Bart Starr," said many fans, "is a so-so quarterback. He can't throw the long bomb the way Unitas does. And he doesn't gamble. You could guess what play Starr is going to call and be right seventy per cent of the time. What's more, what quarterback wouldn't look good with runners like Hornung and Taylor? If he didn't have Hornung and Taylor, Starr would have to throw long passes. If he did, he'd be in trouble."

Starr heard those remarks. He shrugged and said nothing. He knew what he had to do, and after each game the confidence surged inside him.

The next Sunday Bart walked into Wrigley Field to play the Bears. Early in the game he darted back to pass. He knew the Bear defense liked to shift around a lot. He stood in the pocket, waiting for the defense to form.

It formed and now Starr could "read" it, as the quarterbacks say. What he read he liked. He saw, from what he read, that Boyd Dowler should be free on the left side. Bart arrowed a pass to Dowler, who grabbed the pass all alone and galloped twenty-five yards downfield.

Moments later, standing over the center, barking out the signals, Starr saw the Bear defense overload to the left side. "They're going to shoot a linebacker in on me," Bart realized. Quickly he changed the play, calling an automatic.

Listening to the automatic, Paul Hornung got the message. He was supposed to circle over the middle. On the signal, Hornung faked a block on a lineman, circled the end and raced to the spot vacated by that linebacker who was now shooting in on Starr.

Hornung turned and saw the football whistling toward him. He grabbed the ball out of the air, turned, and ran thirty-five yards, untouched, into the end zone.

All afternoon long Starr penetrated the Bear defense, angling passes to open receivers, firing his runners through wide-open holes. The final score was Green Bay 41, Chicago 13. The

Packers had pushed the Bears out of the race. But Green Bay still trailed Baltimore.

In the winner's clubhouse, Lombardi cracked a smile. "We played a real good game," he said. "But now we have to hope Detroit can beat Baltimore today. Does anyone know the score?"

"Yes," said a reporter. "Baltimore is leading, 15-13, with less than a minute to go."

Lombardi winced. "We have to hope that someone beats the Colts. If not, we're out of it."

Someone asked him about Starr. "Bart's calls were really perfect," he said. "A coach can't send in plays against the Bears' defense because you never know what it will be. It is very complicated. The quarterback often has to call an automatic, and Starr's automatics were perfect."

A writer ran into the room, breathing hard. "The Lions scored on the last play of the game," he yelled. "They beat the Colts, 20-15."

"Are you sure?" said Lombardi, his eyes widening. "Don't tell the players if you're not sure."

"I'm sure," said the man.

"How about that?" shouted Lombardi. "Now we're tied with the Colts for first place."

Each team had two games left — both on the west coast, both against the same two clubs, the San Francisco 49ers and the Los Angeles Rams.

The following weekend, playing on a muddy field at San Francisco, Taylor and Hornung slogged through the goo to score one touchdown and set up two field goals by Hornung. The Packers won, 13-0. In Los Angeles the Rams beat the Colts, 10-3.

"*We're in first place!*" yelled the happy

Packers in the clubhouse, mud splattered over their faces.

"O.K.! O.K.!" Lombardi yelled over the din. At the sound of his voice the room went quiet, the Packers staring respectfully at their coach. "But next week we got to win again. We don't want any tie and a playoff. Right?"

"Right!" yelled the Packers.

The following Saturday the Packers played the Rams in Los Angeles. Three hours before game time, the Packers boarded the bus outside their hotel. "O.K.," hollered an assistant coach in the front of the bus. "It's time to go."

"Wait," said a Packer player. "Starr and Knafelc aren't here yet."

Bart and his roommate, end Gary Knafelc, had been delayed getting out of their room. Two minutes after the bus had been scheduled to leave, they raced up the street. They jumped into the bus.

Lombardi's voice cut through the air with the snap of a whip. "That'll cost you $25 each," he said in his cutting tone.

Starr looked down at his feet. All the players in the bus, as well as the newspapermen, everyone had heard. Here he was, the quarterback of the team, being fined for being late.

His ears flamed red, but he said nothing. He took his seat. He had been wrong. He had delayed the bus. Some players might have sulked. Not Bart Starr.

That afternoon he fired eight straight passes before the dazzled Rams batted down one of his throws. When the Rams jammed up the center to stop Taylor and Hornung, Starr lobbed passes over the middle, passing for 201 yards and two touchdowns. The Packers won, 35-21.

They ran off the field Western Conference champions. Two years ago they had been losers and now they were winners, champions — *Western Conference champions!*

The Packers flew home to Green Bay to be met by cheering fans. They cheered for Hornung, they cheered for Taylor, they cheered for the defense. And they cheered for Bart Starr. "Beautiful game, Bart," hollered one man as Bart came down the steps of the airplane. "You were terrific!"

"Hey," said a man next to him. "I thought you were a Lamar McHan man."

"Not any more," said the fan. "In Green Bay tonight, everybody is a Bart Starr man."

In the National Football League the Western Conference champion meets the Eastern Conference champion for the league title. In 1960 the Philadelphia Eagles were Eastern champions.

On December 26th, a gray and sullen day in Philadelphia, the Packers lined up against the Eagles. This was a tough, spirited Philadelphia team, led by quarterback Norm Van Brocklin on offense and hard-tackling Chuck Bednarik on defense.

At the half the Eagles led 10-6. All through the third period the two great defensive units hurled back Starr and Van Brocklin. As the fourth period began, Philadelphia still led, 10-6.

Now the lights of Franklin Field glowed, white and ghostly, through a clammy fog billowing over the gridiron. Despite the fog, Starr went back to pass. He threw to Max McGee for

a first down on the Eagle forty-five. He threw to
Hornung for another first down on the twenty.
Two plays later, the ball on the Eagle thirteen,
Starr danced back, looked through the mist and
saw Ron Kramer angling toward the end zone.
Bart whipped a streaking pass to Kramer, who
caught the ball on the goal line and toppled
across.

Touchdown! The Packers led, 13-10, and now
time was running out on the Eagles. There were
fewer than five minutes left to play.

The Packers kicked off. Eagle rookie Ted Dean
snagged the ball on his own goal line, then did
a little hesitation step, waiting for a wall of
blockers to form what coaches call a "chute."
Up that chute shot Dean, zooming all the way
downfield to the Packer thirty-nine. From there
Norm Van Brocklin steered the fired-up Eagle
backs through the tiring Green Bay defense.
From the five Ted Dean wiggled his way across
the goal line and Philadelphia led, 17-13.

The clock showed a minute and a half left to
play. The ball was deep in Packer territory, a
long eighty yards from the goal line. Starr
kneeled inside the Packer huddle. He shook a
fist, telling the Packers: *We can win this!*

On the play Star winged a short pass, the receiver catching the ball and running out of
bounds to stop the clock. Starr threw another
short pass. And another, completing each one of
these clutch passes as the big minute hand
swept toward zero.

There was time for one last play, the ball inside the Eagle twenty. Bart scanned the Eagle
defense. These were the closing moments of a

championship game, but Bart's face was as calm
as though it were a preseason scrimmage. He
knew what he had to do: He had to complete a
short pass to one of his running backs, prefer-
ably big Jim Taylor. Then he had to hope that
the back and his blockers could bulldoze their
way into the end zone.

Starr stepped back to pass, the big Philadelphia crowd standing and screaming. He threw
a whizzing pass that Jim Taylor grabbed on the
nine-yard line. Taylor lunged toward the goal
line, knees churning. The huge Chuck Bednarik
smashed into him. Jim Taylor's body bent as
Bednarik hit him, but he didn't go down. For
several seconds the two huge bodies swayed in
the fog. And as they battled, like two dinosaurs
on a steamy prehistoric swamp, the game
swayed with them.

Suddenly, out of the mist, flew the bullet-like
bodies of three Philadelphia tacklers, slamming
into Jim Taylor, and down he crashed. The gun
sounded. The game was over. The Philadelphia
Eagles were National Football League champions.

The Packers walked off the field after shaking
hands with the Eagles. They had come close,
within nine yards and another minute, to winning that championship. But football fields are
one hundred yards long, not ninety-one. And
football games are played in sixty minutes, not
sixty-one. The Packers had come close, but not
close enough.

In the clubhouse Starr slumped on a rubdown
table, his green shirt and gold pants smeared
with mud. A jagged cut ran, bloody red, across

his nose. "Almost," said someone to him. He had thrown thirty-five passes and completed twenty-one. Not one of his passes had been intercepted, and one completion had gone for a touchdown.

Starr looked up. "Almost," he said with a sad smile, "isn't good enough."

He stood, wincing from a hundred bruises. "I'll tell you," he said through gritted teeth. "This year we won the Western title but lost to the East. Next year we're going to win that Western title again. And then — look out, East!"

8

"We Had It In Our Hearts"

THE PHONE RANG IN Bart Starr's living room. The time was a day late in March of 1961. Bart Starr came into the room and picked up the phone, shucking off a leather jacket.

"Yes, I know," he said over the phone. "I heard about it. I sure wish Lamar all the good luck in the world. He is a fine person and a fine quarterback."

Bart hung up the phone. Someone had just called to tell him the news: Vince Lombardi had traded his No. Two quarterback, Lamar McHan, to the Washington Redskins. Now there could be no doubt — Bart Starr was the Packers' No. One quarterback.

A few weeks earlier Starr had had reason to wonder if he was No. One. In the newspapers, columnists had written that Vince Lombardi had offered any two Packers for the Dallas Cowboys' talented young quarterback, Don Meredith. According to the stories, Lombardi was unhappy with Starr. He had been very unhappy after the 1960 championship game, said the writers. He had watched the crafty Norm

Van Brocklin steer the Eagles to a victory he thought the Packers should have won. What Lombardi needed to win that championship, said the writers, was a smarter quarterback. Before the 1961 season began, they wrote, Lombardi would get that quarterback — and right now he had his eyes on Don Meredith.

Then flashed news of the trade. McHan had been sent to the Redskins. That killed all the rumors about Meredith coming to the Packers. When Lombardi traded his No. Two quarterback, he was telling the league emphatically: Bart Starr is my No. One quarterback.

Bart had to be pleased. "The trade really gave me the confidence I needed," he said at the Packers' 1961 summer camp. "I know that the coach is willing to go with me alone. Things haven't bothered me the way they used to. Some years ago, if I threw an interception, even here at camp, I'd brood about it. Or if I made a bad call, I'd let it bother me. That only made things worse. Now, after an interception or a bad call, I forget them. But I know I'd better rectify my mistake. Quick."

In the 1961 preseason games, Bart Starr made few mistakes and the Packers won all five. Then came Opening Day and another shock. The Lions ripped by Bart's blockers and knocked him down time after time. The Lions won, 17-13.

Green Bay won its next game, walloping the 49ers, 30-10. In restaurants and hotel lobbies in Green Bay the next week, the fans sat with players like Jim Taylor, Boyd Dowler, and Ray Nitschke. On street corners they chatted with Jim Ringo and Starr. "Next week is the big one,"

BART STARR

Power and versatility. The flexibility of the Packers'
running attack is frighteningly evident in this action
shot taken during the 1966 NFL championship game
against the Dallas Cowboys. As offensive blockers
open the Dallas line, Bart Starr (15) has just
completed a handoff to Elijah Pitts (22). Although the
play is committed, Jim Taylor (31) represented
another potential threat to the Cowboy defense
moving from right to left in the backfield. Green Bay
won, 34-27.

Packer coach Vince Lombardi manages a smile near the
end of the 1965 NFL title game against the Cleveland
Browns. (The game was actually played on January 2,
1966.) Bart Starr, a doubtful starter early in the week,
led Green Bay to a 23-12 victory.

SOMETIMES IT WORKS . . .
In the first Super Bowl game against Kansas City,
Starr hands off to Elijah Pitts (22) for yardage on
a running play (below).
Bart Starr's pass barely escapes the reach of the
Chiefs' Buck Buchanan (86) in the Super Bowl—but
it's complete to Max McGee for a touchdown
(next page).

SOMETIMES IT DOESN'T . . .
A bad moment during the 1967 Super Bowl. Smothering
Starr for a seven-yard loss in the third quarter are
Kansas City linebacker Ed Holub (55) and defensive
tackle Buck Buchanan (86). In front of Starr is Forrest
Gregg (75).

In a defense-dominated 1965 game against the Dallas
Cowboys, Bart Starr is thrown for a six-yard loss by
end Maury Youmans (78) and tackle Bob Lilly (74).
Held for only seventy-three yards rushing and
passing, Green Bay nonetheless won, 13-3.

And sometimes you lose. Bart Starr slumps on the sidelines at Green Bay after his pass was intercepted by the Baltimore Colts to stop a drive in the final minutes. The Colts won this second game of the 1964 season 21-20, and went on to take the Western Conference title.

the fans said to the players. "We play the Bears. Don't you figure we have to beat the Bears to win the Western Conference championship?"

"I'd say so," said Taylor. "If we can beat the Bears twice and the Lions the one other time we get to play 'em, I'd say we have a real good chance."

That Sunday the big bad Bears shot Bill George through the Packers' line. George's elbow smashed into Bart Starr's face, bloodying his lip. But Bart the Cool wiped the blood off his mouth, then threw a touchdown pass to Boyd Dowler. The Packers rolled to an easy 24-0 victory.

The Packers won six in a row before an old nemesis, Johnny Unitas, passed them silly in Baltimore. The Colts won, 45-21. The next week, though, the Packers did what Jim Taylor said they had to do. They beat the Bears in a thriller, 31-28. On Thanksgiving Day their turkey tasted heavenly for they avenged that Opening Day loss to the Lions, beating Detroit, 17-9.

The Packers were on their way to winning in the west. In the east the New York Giants were on their way to winning the Eastern Conference title. It looked like the Giants would play the Packers in the 1961 championship game. As chance would have it, the two teams were scheduled to play each other near the close of the season. The game would be a preview of the championship game.

That 1961 Giant team came to Milwaukee with two crafty quarterbacks. There was Charlie Conerly, the Gray Fox, playing the last season of a long and distinguished career. And there was Y. A. Tittle. The Bald Eagle, the Giants called him; when he took off his helmet, his hairless scalp glistened in the sun.

The Giants boasted a stubborn defense, anchored by their middle linebacker, Sam Huff. Their pass umbrella had, as its spokes, fleet men like Dick Lynch and Jim Patton.

Bart Starr, though, outslicked the Giant defense, throwing passes for short gains, then punching Jim Taylor over tackle when the linebackers dropped back. The Packers won, 20-17.

In New York, Giant fans only smiled. They knew that the Giants were the kind of a team tough to beat twice. "You beat the Giants once," said the New York fans. "But the Giants go away, after you have beaten them, knowing your weaknesses. Then they come back to tear into those weaknesses and rip you apart.

"Our older players, like Tittle and Huff and Lynch, they learned a lot playing the Packers. Just wait until you see what happens when we play them for real — for the NFL championship."

Several weeks later the Giants won the Eastern Conference title, and the Packers won their second straight Western Conference title. On an icy cold day the Giants arrived in Green Bay for the championship game the next afternoon.

Everywhere they saw signs hanging in store windows. The signs read: "Titletown, U.S.A." The citizens of Green Bay were boasting that their little city soon would be the capital of all pro football.

"Hah," said one Giant when he saw the signs. "You've got that spelled wrong."

"What do you mean?" said an indignant Green Bay citizen. "Titletown. That's the way to spell it."

"No, sir," said the Giant, grinning. "It should be spelled this way. T-i-t-t-l-e-town. Because when Y. A. Tittle gets through throwing against the Packers, you'll have to name this little city after Tittle."

And the Giant player laughed.

Tittle and Conerly, together, had been throwing passes in pro football games for close to thirty years. As one Giant fan claimed, "Tittle and Conerly have forgotten more plays than young Bart Starr knows."

One play of Starr's, though, had worked very well in the first game against the Giants. It was an off-tackle slant, with Jim Taylor bulling his big shoulders through the right side of the Giant line.

The Giants came west prepared to stop those slants by Taylor. In fact, the entire Giant defense was keyed up to stop Taylor. The Giants knew that Paul Hornung had been in the Army most of the last half of the season. Paul would be back for the championship game but with only a week's practice. The Golden Boy did not figure to be running with his usual zig-zag sharpness. To make Green Bay's chances even gloomier, Taylor was limping on a sore leg.

When the game began, the Giants' coach, Allie Sherman, threw up a surprise defense — a five-man front line. Twice Starr sent Taylor and Hornung hurtling into that five-man line, and twice the two big backs were flung back for little or no gain.

In the huddle Starr peered out at the Giant defense. He was thinking in that quick, computer-like way of his. Then, looking up at the Packers, he called the play.

On the snap Bart wheeled and handed off to Hornung. Two guards pulled out of the Packer line, and suddenly four men were running interference for Hornung. The four blockers, as big and fast as baby elephants, knocked down the left side of the Giant line, and out into the clear popped Hornung. He ran twenty yards downfield before a Giant safetyman caught up to tackle him.

The Giants quickly shifted back into a four-man line. If they didn't, Sherman knew, Starr would go on wiping out that line with his screen of blockers, freeing the runner for a ten- or twenty-yard gallop up the middle.

Despite that run by Hornung, the Giants still were looking for Starr to hand off to Taylor. Hornung, the Giants still figured, would be rusty after all those months in the army.

Starr, though, had other ideas. "First," he said after the game, "Taylor was hurt so he wasn't up to his full effectiveness. Then Hornung had looked good last week in our workouts. Even though he had missed a lot of practice, he was crisp and sharp. I had made up my mind — and I'm sure coach Lombardi felt the same way — that I'd use Paul a lot more."

Neither team scored in the first period. But early in the second period Starr took the Packers to the Giant six-yard line.

Six yards to go for a touchdown! The grim-

faced Giant defense lined up to stop the
Packers. In the Giants' defensive huddle, Huff
said, "Look out for Taylor." Huff remembered
how Taylor had slanted through the Giant line
in that first game. As the Packers came out of the
huddle, Huff stationed himself slightly to the
right of the middle of the line.

Starr, in an instant, "read" what Huff was doing. Huff had stationed himself smack in the
pathway of Taylor's slant play off tackle — the
play that had worked so well in the first game.

Starr's face was impassive as he scanned the
Giant defense, not even a twitch of the lip in-
dicating he saw what Huff had done. His voice
rang out in the cold air. "Thirty-seven, sixty-
two. . . ." On the snap he faked a handoff to
Taylor, and the Giants slammed into the big
fullback.

"The left . . . the left . . . ," a Giant player
was hollering. He saw that Starr, after faking to
Taylor, had given the ball to Hornung. But
Hornung zipped through the wide-open left side
of the Giant line and raced into the end zone for
a touchdown.

"Anytime a defense makes a change," said
Starr after the game, "they have to give up something. We try to find that something."

Within the next ten minutes, Starr would find
a lot of somethings.

Moments after Hornung scored, the Packers
picked off a Tittle pass. Starr directed the team
to the Giant thirteen. From there he stepped
back to throw a high arching pass that rangy
Boyd Dowler ran under in the end zone.
Green Bay led, 14-0.

Five minutes later, the ball rested on the

Giant fourteen. From inside his huddle, Starr stared at the Giant defense. On the previous play he had noticed that Huff had moved slightly out of position at middle linebacker. Again Huff had been looking for that off-tackle slant by Taylor.

Starr suspected something. If a flood of Packer receivers showed up on Huff's right, figured Starr, Huff would spring to his right to cover the receivers.

"Flood right," whispered Starr. The Packers clapped hands and leaped out of the huddle.

On the snap three receivers flooded the right side, looping and looking back for a pass from Starr. On the left side, Ron Kramer slammed into two of the Giant cornerbacks. They flung him away, dashing to the right — along with Huff — to cover that flood of receivers. They were sure Kramer was blocking. He couldn't possibly be going out for a pass.

But Kramer *was* going out for a pass. He raced to the spot left open by Huff, caught a pass thrown by Starr, then bowled over two tacklers as he toppled into the end zone.

Touchdown! The Packers led, 21-0. The Giant defense walked, as though numbed, off the field. Starr twice had run plays at the heart of the Giant defense — at Sam Huff — and twice had scored touchdowns.

"If you beat a team at its strongest point," Lombardi often told the Packers, "you'll win because you'll destroy its morale." Now Starr was beating the Giants at their strongest point — Sam Huff — and the Giant defense was beginning to doubt itself. "If he can fool Sam," the players said to themselves, "what chance have I got against this guy?"

In the third period, ahead now 24-0, Starr called another "flood right." This time the Giants picked up Kramer, Joe Morrison covering him as he raced toward the spot left open by Huff.

The cool and methodical Starr was thinking step by step with the Giants. He faked a pass to Kramer, who then broke to the outside corner of the end zone, away from Morrison. Starr dropped another long pass into his arms.

Touchdown! The Packers now led, 31-0. In the fourth period Paul Hornung kicked a field goal and then the Packers let the clock run out.

Bang! The gun sounded, ending the game. And with that *bang!* thousands of Green Bay fans stood and cheered and cheered. This *was* Titletown, U.S.A. The Packers, at long last, *were* champions of the National Football League.

Down on the field his players picked up Vince Lombardi. They carried him off the field, swaying on their broad shoulders. And the crowd cheered until their throats were raw and dry.

In only three years, a team of losers had become a team of champions. As the Packers ducked down into the concrete tunnels under the stadium, yelling as they ran to their clubhouse, they could hear that crowd cheering. Green Bay was telling its Packers: Well done, boys, well done.

In the clubhouse a huge, wet-eyed Willie Davis, a giant on defense, told reporters how much this meant to the Packers. "We have had it in our hearts to prove ourselves since the championship game last year," he said. "We all

knew there shouldn't have been any way for the
Eagles to beat us last year."

In a corner of the room, Vince Lombardi held
up his hands. Immediately the Packers stopped
their yelling, turning to look at their coach.

For a moment Lombardi was silent, the hush
in the room as heavy as the steamy air. Then,
in that raspy voice of his, Lombardi told it all
to his team:

"Today," he said, "you were the best team in
the history of the National Football League."

In the Giant clubhouse the wise old Conerly,
who had played his last NFL game, tugged off
a jersey. "That Starr," he said in his Mississippi
drawl, "he sure was something. How many did
he complete out there today?"

A writer looked at a mimeographed sheet of
statistics. "Well," said the writer, "he threw
seventeen and completed ten of them for three
touchdowns. And he had no interceptions."

"You can't hardly do much better than that,
can you?" said the graying veteran, smiling
weakly.

"Bart Starr performed like a champion," Vince
Lombardi was saying. "He called the plays and
made the offensive changes that were needed.
He knows exactly what I want. He follows our
ready sheet for a game perfectly. We win because we make very, very few mistakes."

A ring of reporters clustered around Hornung.
He had scored a record nineteen points. "Sure,"
said an assistant coach, watching the writers
question Hornung. "Hornung was spectacular.
But the key man for us was Bart Starr."

The key man sat on a stool, ignored by the

writers. His dirt-smeared pants were wadded at his ankles. A single reporter, noticing him, came over to talk. "Well," said the writer, "how does it feel to be the youngster who outsmarted the two old pros — Conerly and Tittle?"

"Oh, no, sir," said Starr, looking up quickly. "I didn't try to match wits with them. No, sir. We won as a team. In Green Bay we don't have any individual stars."

In triumph, as in defeat, Bart was still Bart the Cool.

9

A Day in the Lions' Den

VINCE LOMBARDI STOOD
up in the clubhouse. The Packer players watched
him, seated on stools, their shoulder pads bulg-
ing under green jerseys.

This was the first day of 1962 summer camp
for the Packers. A sign above the clubhouse
read: "Green Bay Packers — 1961 World
Champions." On a wall in the clubhouse a player
had scrawled this challenge: "We did it in 1961,
we can do it in 1962."

Lombardi looked around the room. "This is
going to be a tough year for us," he growled.
"This season everyone is going to be up to beat
us. We won the Western Conference title in
1960, we won it again in 1961. They can't take
that away from us. But a lot of people — the
Colts, the Bears, the Lions — they are going to
try as hard as they can to beat us this season."

The coach stared at his players. "Are you
going to let them take that title away from us?"

"*No!*" roared his players. A few minutes later
they charged out onto the practice field, ready
to start drilling for the 1962 season.

At the end of that 1962 season, Starr slumped

in a chair in the living room of the house he had
bought in Green Bay. "It was a tough year, exactly as coach Lombardi said it would be," he
said. "Everybody was laying for us. Every week
was a dog fight. We had to be up for each one
of the thirteen games."

One day during the preseason drills at the
1962 summer camp, Starr set a personal goal
for himself. In 1961 only sixteen of his 295 passes
had been intercepted — an excellent percentage. But Starr figured he could cut down on the
passes he threw to the wrong people. "It kills
you to give up the ball," he said. "If you don't
have the ball in this game, you can't score. I'm
hoping to throw a lot fewer interceptions."

Later that afternoon, after practicing tosses
to his receivers, Starr sat in front of his locker in
the clubhouse. Sweat streaked his face, and he
looked tired. But, as usual, he was happy to
talk football.

"The great thing about coach Lombardi," he
was saying, "is that he really gets you ready for
a game. He repeats and repeats. Finally you can
recognize the other team's defenses in your
sleep. Lombardi gets you ready. He gives you
the confidence you've got to have going into a
game."

Starr was confident as he stood on the sideline before the opening kickoff of the 1962 opening game. But, as usual, he was nervous. On the
other side of the field, the Minnesota Vikings
warmed up. In the stands some fifty thousand
Green Bay fans thundered applause as each
Packer ran out onto the field to be introduced.

A minute later, the game under way, Green

Bay had the ball. Starr ducked into the huddle.
He called a play, then trotted up to the line of
scrimmage with his team. As he stood there,
scanning the defense, he still felt the tension
churning inside him. Then he took the snap and
handed off to Jim Taylor. He heard the *crack!
crack! crack!* as pads smacked into pads, the
grunts and yells of the linemen, the pounding
of cleats on ground. He turned to watch the ball
carrier and the tension began to drain out of
him. A few plays later, all the tension gone, he
was handing off, faking, throwing passes with
the smoothness of a well-oiled machine.

The well-balanced Packer offense buried the
Vikings, 34-7. The next week the Packers toppled
the Cardinals, 17-0. They roared by the Bears,
49-0. The Lions came to Green Bay and, as
usual, threw a strong rush at Starr. But Paul
Hornung kicked three field goals and the
Packers won, 9-7.

"Detroit," said Starr after the game. "That's
the team we're going to have to beat out if we're
going to win the Western Conference title this
year."

In the Lions' dressing room, Joe Schmidt,
then the Detroit defensive captain, shook his
head. "That Starr," he said, "he's so cool out
there. Nothing seems to ruffle him. You can
never get him mad, and that's what we like to
do. Get the quarterback all excited or mad. You
can hit him as hard as you can, he never seems
to lose his cool."

"Bart Starr knows exactly what I want,"
Lombardi was saying. "He follows our ready
lists for a game perfectly."

Someone asked Starr what a ready list was.

"For each game," he said, "the coaches give the quarterbacks a ready list — several running plays to each hole off each formation. And a few passing plays off each formation. There are a half dozen or so plays the coaches think should be most effective against that week's opponent.

"I don't know how many plays we have altogether in our playbook. I've never counted them. But there are a whole lot of them. We have these plays in reserve for a game. But we rarely need them. The half dozen or so plays on our ready list, plays that should work against an opponent, usually do."

The Packers' ready lists were working just fine. Until Thanksgiving Day of the 1962 season, the Packers had run off a string of ten straight victories without a defeat.

The Thanksgiving Day game was played in Detroit's cavernous Tiger Stadium on a cold and windy morning. The first time the Packers had the ball, 275-pound Alex Karras and 300-pound Roger Brown flew by the Packer blockers and smacked Starr to the ground.

They knocked him down all game long, the Lion fans roaring on each tackle. Groggy, Starr slowly got to his feet each time, weaving back to the huddle to call another play.

In the second half, behind by two touchdowns, Starr desperately searched his ready list for a play that would work against the blitzing Lions. With the ball on his own forty-two, Starr figured the linebackers would blitz in on him on the next play.

"O.K.," he said to the Packers in the huddle. "We'll catch them blitzing this time."

He called for a hook-in pass. Ron Kramer would circle from his tight-end spot into an area left bare by a blitzing linebacker.

Starr stepped up over the center. From the corner of his eye he saw Lion linebacker Wayne Walker edge up to the line.

Starr watched, delighted inside, but keeping his face impassive. This was just what he wanted — Walker to blitz in on him, leaving Kramer free. If Starr could complete a pass against the blitz, he'd worry the Lions into calling off the blitzing.

Starr barked out the signals. He grabbed the snap from the center and darted back. He looked to see where Wayne Walker was. He bit his lip in frustration. Walker wasn't blitzing. He was dropping back, glued to Ron Kramer.

Bart looked to find another receiver. Nobody was open. Around him, amid the grunts of his blockers and the yells of a thundering charge of Lions, he could see his pocket crumbling. A hand grabbed at him. Bart twisted away. Suddenly a flaring light exploded in his head and down he dropped, hit on the side of the helmet by a charging Lion's fist.

He got up, dazed, shaking his head. Soon the Lions were charging for another touchdown. They won the game easily, 26-14. In the clubhouse after the game, a bruised and bloodied Starr smiled wanly at a friend. "It was one of those games," he said. "No matter what you do, the other side is always a play ahead of you."

He looked up, confidence showing as he smiled. "But we're still one game ahead of them," he said. "They've lost two. We've lost only one. We've got only three games to play.

If we win all three, it doesn't matter what Detroit does. We win the Western Conference title."

The following week Green Bay beat the Rams. But Detroit also won. The Packers still led by one game.

The following Sunday that thin lead was evaporating to nothing. The Packers were playing in San Francisco's Kezar Stadium. At the half they trudged off to their clubhouse, losing 21-10. And as they looked up at the scoreboard, the Packers saw that the Lions had won.

In Detroit, fans bit their nails. They hovered near their radios. If the 49ers could hold onto the lead and beat the Packers, the Lions would be tied and there might have to be a playoff. In that playoff, the Lions — always tough for the Packers — figured to be favorites.

In the Packer clubhouse, Lombardi looked at his players. "All right," he said, his voice cracking through the room. "If we lose, maybe we will have a playoff on our hands. We don't want any playoff. Now all you fellows on defense, let's get in there and hit them. Stop pussyfooting. And you fellows on offense, let's get some points on the scoreboard."

Starr came out for the second half in that sauntering way he has once the tension is gone. "He looks," said a writer in the press box, "like he was ahead 21-10 instead of being behind 21-10."

On the first play of the half, Starr called for a pass. He threw. *Complete!* He handed off to Jim Taylor, who ran for a first down. He threw again. *Complete!* Then he handed off to Hornung, who circled the end on the Packers' power sweep, led by an armada of blockers. Hornung dashed into the end zone.

Up went the referee's arms. *Touchdown!* But the Packers still trailed 21-17. A few minutes later the Packers took over again near midfield. Starr dashed back and threw. The ball arrowed between the fingers of two defenders. *Complete!* He handed off to Hornung, then to Taylor.

Up the field, toward the 49ers' goal line, crunched the Green Bay machine. "Bart Starr," said Norm Van Brocklin, the old quarterback, "kills you with those nickel-and-dime passes. And the Packers never let loose of the ball with that three-four-move-the-yardage-sticks offense. Bart Starr is cool. He's the master of all situations."

The cool Starr, throwing those short nickel-and-dime passes and picking up three, four, and six yards with handoffs to Taylor and Hornung, marched past the twenty, past the fifteen, past the ten, then ploughed into the end zone.

Touchdown! The Packers led, 24-21. Minutes later they scored another touchdown and ran off the field, pounding each other on the backs. They had won, 31-21, and now they were sure of at least a tie for the Western Conference title.

The next week, the final week of the season, Green Bay won again. Vince Lombardi and the Packers had won their third successive Western Conference title.

And Bart Starr had a private victory. Before the season began, he had set a personal goal: to reduce his number of interceptions.

The year before he had thrown sixteen interceptions in 295 attempts. Now, in 1962, he put the ball in the air almost the same number

of times — a total of 285. Only nine were intercepted.

Then came the 1962 championship game —
the Packers against their foes of a year earlier,
the Giants, the same team Green Bay had hum-
bled, 37-0, in Green Bay.

This game would be played in New York's
Yankee Stadium before some sixty-five thousand
Giant fans screaming for revenge. The fans carried banners titled: "Beat Green Bay" and "Remember 1961."

Those banners soon were frozen stiff. Fifty-
mile-an-hour winds swirled over the field, with
the temperature at a frigid fifteen degrees. The
fans in the stands huddled, shivering, under
parkas and thick overcoats.

Out on the middle of the frozen, grassless
field, Starr tried to warm up. He clapped his
hands together to get feeling into his fingers.
"The wind was what made it so cold," he said
later. "We've practiced in ten-below-zero
weather in Green Bay and it wasn't as cold as it
felt in New York."

Early in the game the Giants' Y. A. Tittle
threw a short pass to Del Shofner as Del cut to
the sideline. The ball zipped toward Shofner,
then suddenly dropped like a stone. The swirling wind had caught the ball and batted it to
the ground like some invisible fist.

For most of the first period, Starr stuck to
running plays. "I don't like to pass out there,"
he told an assistant coach on the sideline. "You
can't tell what the wind will do with the ball. It
could blow it into the wrong pair of hands."

Calling straight-ahead running plays and
power sweeps to the left or right, Starr steered

the Packers to the Giant twenty-six. There, though, the big New York defense held. Earlier in the season Hornung's leg had been injured. Ron Kramer had replaced him as the Packers' field-goal kicker. With Starr kneeling to hold the ball, Kramer took two quick steps forward and booted the ball high into the dark sky.

The players turned to stare as the ball soared, end over end, toward the goal posts. Up went the referee's arms. The kick was good. Green Bay led, 3-0.

"Go-oh, Giii-ants!" chanted the New York fans as the Giant offense ran out onto the field. Y. A. Tittle had the ball on the Giant twenty-eight. He handed off to a runner, who took two steps forward.

Whomp! A Green Bay lineman dropped him. The ball squirted loose, spinning on the ground. A Green Bay player fell on the ball. In rushed the Packer offense.

"One thing I like to do after a team fumbles," said Bart later, "is to come right back with something and hit 'em. It's not like after a punt. The defense has got to be unsettled after a fumble. They've come into the game unexpectedly, without having a chance to get ready."

In the huddle Starr called a Packer favorite. The players looked at Starr, a little surprised. A pass? In the wind? But this, they realized, was a pass born out of surprise.

Starr took the snap, turned, and handed off to Paul Hornung. Up rushed a Giant cornerback to nail Hornung. The Golden Boy stopped and threw a pass over the head of the cornerback. The pass bounced in the wind, but it dropped into Boyd Dowler's arms on the Giant seven, where he was tackled.

"Let's hold 'em," the Giant defense hollered at each other as the Packers lined up for the next play. But they looked confused, upset by that surprise pass from a halfback.

Bart took the snap, handing off to Jim Taylor. The stumpy broad-shouldered fullback roared out of the arms of two Giant tacklers, popped into daylight and barreled the seven yards into the end zone. Kramer kicked the extra point and the Packers led, 10-0.

"I thought that play might work," Starr said on the sideline. "It was aimed for the right side, and I think we caught Sam Huff guessing we were going left. There was nobody where he should have been, and Taylor had a clear alley to the end zone."

In the second half Starr moved the Packers "close enough in," as the quarterbacks say, for Kramer to kick another two field goals. The Giants scored one touchdown by blocking a kick in the end zone. But Y. A. Tittle could not get the frozen Giant offense to move on that dark, icy, and wind-swept field.

Suddenly a gun roared, its sound quickly dying away amid the whine of the wind. The Packers turned, grabbed their frozen-cheeked coach and carried him out of Yankee Stadium. They had won, 16-7. The Packers were world champions for the second straight year.

"Are you cold?" said someone to Lombardi in the warm dressing room. "Cold?" barked Lombardi. "I'm not cold." Then he laughed. "You're only cold when you lose."

Starr had thrown twenty-one passes into the

swirling winds. Somehow he had completed nine. None were intercepted.

The writers gathered around him. "I'll bet you'll be glad to leave this freezing weather," said a writer.

"Yes, sir," said Starr. "My next game will be the Pro Bowl game in Los Angeles — where it's nice and warm." He laughed, staring at red, chapped fingers, smeared with dirt and blood.

"Will you be the West's starting quarterback against the East in the Pro Bowl?" asked another writer.

"Why not?" said Starr, looking up. "I think I earned that right."

Bart Starr had earned the right. But he wouldn't start for the West in the Pro Bowl. Johnny Unitas would start. Bart Starr would sit on the bench, angry at someone he knew very well — Vince Lombardi.

10

Who Is Better — Unitas or Starr?

THERE WAS ANGER IN Bart Starr's voice as he talked to the reporters. The reporters had gathered around him on the sideline as the West squad finished drilling for the Pro Bowl Game in Los Angeles' Coliseum. A little earlier in the day, the West's coach, Vince Lombardi, had announced that Johnny Unitas would start for the West.

"How about Starr?" asked a reporter.

"Well," said Lombardi, looking embarrassed, "we have eight Packers on the squad. It wouldn't look right to put too many of them into the starting lineup."

Now the reporters, standing with Starr, were telling him what Lombardi had said. "I know what he said," Starr murmured.

"Does it bother you — not starting?"

"Sure, it bothers me," said Bart, his voice louder. "I went to Coach Lombardi and I told him how I felt. I told him I thought I had earned the right to start. I don't think it was the idea of starting or any glory involved. I couldn't care less. That's beside the point. But I've been on a championship team two years now. If there were ten of us here from the Packers, we merited the right."

"I'll bet," said a writer, "you wouldn't have talked that way to Lombardi a few years ago."

"No," said Starr, a sheepish grin on his face. "A couple of years ago I'd probably have hung my head and looked at my feet."

Starr laughed. He is not the kind to stay angry very long. Unitas did start the game. Late in the game Unitas fumbled. The fumble was picked up by the East, which scored a touchdown and beat the West, 30-20.

Even in defeat, though, a lot of people thought Unitas was a better quarterback than Starr. The former great Bear quarterback, Johnny Lujack, said of Starr: "A good short passer, but only an average long passer. I rate him well in the categories of faking, running, leadership, and play calling. But he has one important weakness. He doesn't throw long passes often enough to keep the defense from packing in tight against Green Bay's running and short-passing games."

In other words, Unitas throws the long pass — the bomb. Starr seldom does.

Then, too, said the critics, Starr called dull and unimaginative plays. Unitas called daring plays. "Starr runs Taylor into the line," they said, "and then he runs Hornung around the ends. He has as much imagination as a robot. And he's only a so-so passer. Sure, he completes a lot of passes. But that's only because the defense has to concentrate on stopping the runs of Hornung and Taylor."

Most pro football players, though, smiled when they heard those comments. To them, Starr and Unitas were two great quarterbacks, but two different types.

"It's like comparing cheese and chalk," said Baltimore's great receiver, Jimmy Orr. "Johnny has freer control of the club, I think. Bart follows a fairly strict game plan. But he is a brilliant play caller. Johnny gambles more. We're more of a gambling team. I've seen John throw a ball into a spot you'd think no one would throw to and get away with it. But Starr calls a beautiful game. When we're in trouble, John usually throws. When Green Bay is in trouble, Starr can do anything — run or throw, call a draw play that surprises the defenses."

"He's confident," said a Bear lineman. "You can't ruffle him. You can't make him mad. He's got more confidence than almost anyone."

Johnny Unitas smiled when people claimed he was a better quarterback than Starr. "We're different types," he once told Tex Maule of *Sports Illustrated*. "Bart's an excellent quarterback but he calls plays to control the ball. I gamble. I throw anytime. But he's a fine passer. Look at his statistics."

Starr doesn't smile when he hears people say he isn't as good a quarterback as Unitas. In private, he has told friends he thinks he is at least as good as Unitas. But in his analytical way, he knows what he can do and what he cannot do.

Once, while interviewing Starr for *Sport Magazine*, writer Dave Wolf reminded Starr of what the critics had said: "He's an uncreative automaton. Worse, he's a pedestrian passer who's only effective because the defense must concentrate on runners like Paul Hornung and Jim Taylor."

"I really can't say anything about those comments because they're true," Starr said to Wolf calmly. "We have a great defense which gets us the ball, and I'll be the first to admit that a strong running game helps your passing. Our ball-control offense, which concentrates on rushing plays and shorter passes, is also a help to me. My arm isn't extremely strong. I couldn't throw the bomb all day the way some quarterbacks do. But the medium-range passing is just right. I wouldn't have been able to become the player I am on another team."

The writer, who has watched Starr for many years, disagreed. "As usual," wrote Wolf, "Starr was selling himself short." And Wolf looked up some statistics.

"Through 1964," wrote Wolf, "the Packers usually gained more yardage on the ground than they did in the air. Since then — with Hornung and Taylor less overpowering — they have totaled 3,161 yards rushing and 4,940 yards passing. But they have continued to win."

Summed up Wolf: "Bart Starr's passing has become the strong point of the Green Bay offense."

Wolf recalled a 1966 game. On third and one on his own seventeen-yard line against the 49ers, Starr faked handing off to Elijah Pitts. Then, with the 49er defense rushing in to throw back Pitts, Starr pitched a pass to a loose Carroll Dale who ran all the way for an eighty-three-yard touchdown.

"Isn't it ridiculous," said Wolf, "to call you uncreative?"

Starr shrugged. "I don't let those remarks

bother me," he said. "I'll say this, though. We create when we call audibles."

Well It is Starr, no one else, who calls audibles (or automatics) to change the plays at the line of scrimmage. And it is Starr, and no one else, who must take the blame if he changes the play and the new play doesn't work. But, typically, Bart Starr doesn't say "*I* create when *I* call audibles." He says, "*We* create when *we* call audibles."

Despite that daring call against the 49ers, though, Starr isn't one to take unnecessary risks. "I don't believe in unnecessary risks," he says. "And as long as we're winning, I couldn't care less who they think the best quarterback is."

For the most part, then, Bart Starr is willing to leave the dramatic, long-range "bombs" to Unitas. "That stuff in the long run, I don't think will win for you," he says. "I'm like coach Lombardi. I play it by the book. If you're controlling the ball, moving downfield, I think you can see where an interception can wreck us. As long as we have the ball, the other fellow can't do anything with it."

At the start of the 1966 season, though, Starr was working to make himself a little more daring. "I've tried to play the game a little more recklessly, with a little more abandon," he told someone. "I've always been ultraconservative."

Then he laughed. "But I guess there's a difference between recklessness and carelessness. In an intersquad game a few days ago, I was intercepted four times. That's carelessness."

When outsiders claim Starr is a bad passer, Vince Lombardi's eyes turn steely hard. "I don't know how the story got out that he couldn't throw the long pass," says Lombardi. "In 1966, for example, he threw more bombs than any quarterback in the league."

Lombardi opened a record book. "Look at this," he said. "In 1966 he threw more than a dozen passes over fifty yards for completions." Lombardi laughed. "But far be it from me to argue with people who write that he can't throw long."

That same record book shows that no passer in the history of the National Football League — not Sammy Baugh nor Sid Luckman nor Johnny Unitas nor Norm Van Brocklin — completed a higher percentage of passes over his career than Bart Starr.

That same record book also shows that no passer in the history of the league had a lower percentage of passes intercepted than Bart Starr.

In 1965 *Sports Illustrated* compared the two great passers — Unitas and Starr — over their careers and over the previous six years:

	Lifetime (1956-65)		Six-year (1960-65)	
	Starr	Unitas	Starr	Unitas
Games	126	125	81	79
Passes	2,069	3,313	1,519	2,184
Completed	1,172	1,811	883	1,200
% Completed	56.6%	54.7%	58.1%	54.9%
Yardage	15,929	26,845	12,268	17,891
Average gain per completion	13.60	14.82	13.89	14.91
Touchdown passes	97	210	56	101
% Intercepted	4.3%	4.5%	3.7%	4.6%

From the table one might draw these conclusions:

1. Unitas is more likely to pass than Starr. This is no surprise, of course. Vince Lombardi prefers his quarterbacks to call runs instead of passes.

2. Starr is the more accurate passer. Again this is no surprise. He throws shorter passes (note the yardage figures) and shorter passes are easier to complete and less likely to be intercepted.

3. Unitas is more likely to pass for a touchdown. The cool and conservative Starr is more likely to keep the ball on the ground inside the twenty and grind his way in.

4. Starr, even though he throws shorter passes, gets about as much yardage out of his pass completions as Unitas. The probable reason: Because he throws less often, Starr is more likely to have a receiver wide open who can run for a long gain.

"As everyone knows," summed up Tex Maule of *Sports Illustrated*, "Unitas is one of the finest quarterbacks of all time. As everyone *should* know, Starr is one of them, too. Starr is the perfect man for the meticulous, grinding Green Bay offense and he has just as much cool and just as much generalship as Unitas."

"If Starr is your quarterback," says a National Football League coach, "you have a guy running your team who won't fumble or throw interceptions or panic — or, at least, he won't do those things too often.

"He'll march your team downfield slowly and steadily, using up time so your defense gets a rest, keeping the ball out of the hands of the other team's offense. That's a ball-control game. But every once in a while, he will throw the long bomb to keep the defense unsure what he's going to do next.

"If Unitas is your quarterback, you are always in the game — even if you are down by three touchdowns with five minutes left. He throws long and short and often. Because he throws so often, he'll be intercepted. That means your defense will have to rush out onto the field. They'll have to work harder. But over a season, Unitas' daring will win a lot of games."

Starr himself doesn't pay much attention to the controversy of who is better — himself or Unitas. "I just do my job," he says in that soft Alabama drawl.

What is that job?

"The quarterback's job," he once said, "is to be a coach on the field. I'd say there are three things a quarterback must have. One, he's got to have the respect of his teammates. Two, his authority must be unquestioned. And three, his teammates must be willing to go to the gates of hell for him."

But how do you get to be that kind of quarterback? Each year Bart Starr talks to groups of boys at football "clinics" and gives them tips on quarterbacking. Let's listen in on the kind of things he says at those clinics.

11

How To Be a Winning Quarterback

"THE BEST ADVICE I CAN give young quarterbacks," Bart Starr once said, "is to tell them to find out all they can about the personnel on their teams. It's very easy to overlook certain kinds of skills in certain kinds of players. You should know your halfbacks, your fullbacks, your ends, your blockers — what they can do and what they cannot do.

"As for passing, if you are a young quarterback, don't try to place hands that aren't fully grown over the entire ball. Simply move your hands close enough to the end to be able to get the grip.

"As you grow older, move the grip gradually more toward the center of the ball until you are gripping it about one third from its end. Most quarterbacks feel most comfortable holding the ball with four fingers across the laces. Hold the ball firmly but don't squeeze it tightly.

"In throwing, don't hold up on the ball and try to guide it. This causes underthrowing and sometimes interceptions. Throw it and then follow through like a baseball pitcher. Johnny

Unitas is an example of a quarterback with a perfect follow through.

"When you call plays, have confidence in your voice. You may have doubt about the play, but you don't want the players to have that doubt. You've got to sound like a marine drill sergeant out there, barking out the plays real loud. If players have this confidence in a play, and if you pick the right blockers and runner to execute the play, you can make the worst play work."

Once Starr had a conversation with Cooper Rollow of the Chicago *Tribune*. They talked about what makes a winning quarterback. "When I am conducting a clinic for boys," said Starr, "I always like to start by talking about attitude. In a nutshell, that's what life is all about. Whether you are playing football or driving a gasoline truck, you get out of life what you put into it. If you have the proper mental attitude, you realize that preparation and desire are essential in achieving a goal. . . .

"Our coach, Vince Lombardi, says that winning isn't everything. But making the *effort* to win *is*. If you work harder than somebody else, chances are you'll beat him though he has more talent than you. *Desire* and *dedication* are everything."

In taking the snap from the center, Starr tells this to young quarterbacks: "The basic thing to consider is comfort. If your position over the center makes you feel awkward or places you under a strain, you're not going to do a good job from the beginning."

Starr suggests that young quarterbacks work with their coach to find the ideal position. Essentially, though, the quarterback should be well balanced, the knees slightly flexed, the weight forward on the balls of the feet.

On the snap, says Starr, the quarterback should take the ball with the laces against the fingertips of the right hand. As soon as the quarterback feels the ball, he should start pulling it toward him. If he waves it to one side or the other, someone might whack it out of his hand. As soon as possible, suggests Starr, pull the ball in toward your midsection.

On a handoff, the quarterback should feed the ball to the running back by "looking" it into the back's arms and midsection. The running back's eyes will be fixed on the hole in the line. It is the quarterback's job to make sure the ball is given to the back without a fumble.

On passes, the quarterback should run back with short steps. Long steps, says Starr, can throw a passer off-balance. And he should never turn his back on the defense as he drops back.

There are two reasons for not turning his back. One, the quarterback will lose sight of the defense and fail to see how it's shifting to guard against the pass. Secondly, he will lose sight of his receivers. It will take him precious time to find them again after he has turned to look downfield.

As he drops back, the passer should keep both hands locked on the ball. "It looks very dramatic to be waving that ball," says Starr. "But hold the ball with both hands to make sure you don't drop it. That can happen very easily, especially if you should bang into one of your own blockers."

In fading back, Starr recommends that most

quarterbacks fade about seven or eight yards into the protective pocket. A quarterback usually can figure that it will take a receiver the same number of seconds to run ten yards downfield as it takes the quarterback to back-pedal seven yards.

In throwing, says Starr, throw overhand. Step forward, the front foot pointing toward the target. As the quarterback releases the ball, the weight shifts from the back leg to the front leg.

To those who worry about pretty spiral passes, Starr says, "Don't worry." He suggests working on a delivery that is natural to the passer. Starr tells young quarterbacks to stand with the knees slightly bent, then take a step forward and throw. "The spiral," he says, "will take care of itself."

But he makes this point: You don't throw a football the way a shotputter heaves the shot. The football is passed, not pushed.

Before calling a play, a quarterback should review the situation. What's the down? How many yards are needed for a first down? Where is the ball on the field? How much time is left to play?

In his talks to young quarterbacks, Starr quickly makes it clear why the pros call him Bart the Cool. "If your receivers are covered," he says, "eat the ball! Never throw to a receiver in a crowd, no matter how tempting the gamble. If you can't throw the ball out of bounds when your receivers are covered, then swallow it."

For young quarterbacks who can't throw footballs a city block, Starr suggests concentrating on accuracy. Practice throwing baseballs or pitching rocks at cans. "Accuracy comes first," says Starr, "distance second."

And he makes this point: "If you don't have the arm for it, don't worry about throwing a 'bomb.' Many a football game has been won with a good short-to-moderate passing game."

Starr tells young quarterbacks at his football clinics to mix running plays with passes. "Don't ever call plays in a pattern so that the defense can guess what you are going to call next. Don't get into habits. On second and ten, for example, you can bet that some quarterbacks are always going to call a pass. When the defense knows a pass is coming, you are in trouble. Once in awhile, on second and ten, such a quarterback would be wise to call a running play. The next time there is a second-and-ten situation, the defense will have to be thinking: Is he going to run or is he going to pass?"

Like any football player — fullback, guard, or center — a quarterback must always be in the best of physical condition. "Stay in shape," says Starr. "I know that the majority of athletes welcome the opportunity to stay fit. But let me point out one thing you may not realize. Do you know that your degree of physical readiness can directly affect your mental frame of mind?"

Then Starr looked back on those days when he sat on the Alabama bench, his back hurting and then not getting to play. "I know this is true because it has happened to me. One of the first things that happen after you lose your physical well being is that you also lose your mental poise. You start worrying about how tired you are and why your legs won't respond, and why your wind seems short. You become preoccupied over your lack of stamina, and you lose your mental sharpness."

A quarterback must have that mental sharpness. "Football is a great game of cat and mouse," he says. "It's a great guessing game. The defense throws something at you to stop something you are doing to it. If it does stop you, then you have to find where it has weakened the defense to stop you. You have to do some guessing to find where it has weakened itself, just as it did some guessing to find out how to stop you.

"There are days when the defense guesses right more often than you do. Those days happen. But don't let changes in the defense rattle you. Just look for where the defense has weakened itself. Then take advantage of that weakness."

Bart Starr directs a simple Green Bay offense. Once Lombardi stood up at a meeting of the Green Bay offensive players. "I can't understand how you make so many mistakes," he growled. "We have a simple offense designed for simpleminded people."

Actually it is only the Green Bay running plays that are fairly simple. The Packer passing attack is complicated. "Our passing attack is different than most people's," says Lombardi. "On lots of teams, the quarterback goes back and one receiver goes out. The quarterback lets go the pass to the one receiver or he eats the ball.

"But we make it a lot tougher for our quarterback. We have option passes with three or four receivers. So when Bart fades back to pass, he has to decide to throw it or eat it not once, not twice, not three times. But four times.

"It's not easy. As he goes back, Bart looks at the defense. He 'reads' the defense, as we say. Sometimes he reads the linebacker, sometimes the safety, sometimes the cornerback. By seeing what they are doing, he usually can tell which receiver should be open."

Of all the passing plays used by the Packers, one special play is Bart's favorite, he once told the Chicago *American*'s Brent Musberger. The play is shown below:

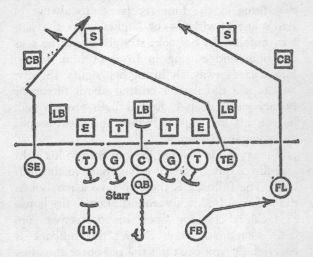

"I like the pass for three reasons," says Starr. "It can be thrown against any defense. There are four good choices of receivers. I can throw to the split end (SE). I can throw to my tight end (TE). I can throw to the flanker (FL). Or I can throw to the fullback (FB).

"The blocking is sound and simple. Big linemen against big defensive linemen. The center is responsible for the middle linebacker. The left halfback is responsible for the linebacker shooting in from his side. And if the linebacker on the fullback's side comes in, the ball is released quickly to the fullback as he flares toward the sideline.

"Another thing I like about this pattern is this: The flanker has a number of routes he can run off his basic move. He can cut in or cut out. He can cut back. He can stop, then take off again on a deep pattern for the bomb."

Take another look at the play. You'll notice that three of the four receivers are always in Bart's line of vision — or "sights" — as the pattern unfolds. As he looks straight ahead he sees the tight end cutting in front of him, ten to fifteen yards away. By lifting his "sights" slightly, he can see the flanker cutting about fifteen or twenty yards deeper. And if both are covered, he can lift his "sights" higher and see his split end going even deeper.

If everyone is covered, he can turn to his right and flip a quick "safety-valve" pass to the fullback. The fullback is there to take a pass when the pressure builds up around Starr — the horde of tacklers cracking open his protective cup. "But sometimes," says Starr, "the fullback is covered. Or you can't get the pass over the arms of a big lineman. That's when you get whacked."

Starr stresses that a quarterback must have the physical toughness to go with his mental sharpness. "Football requires intelligence," says Starr. "But as coach Lombardi says, it is also a game of blocking and tackling. You have got to like the contact to play football real well. Each

year you see boys out to play football in high
school who are unhappy. They don't like the
contact and the violence of football. They'll
never be real good football players. You've got
to love physical contact."

No play in football is more physical than
Green Bay's famous power sweep. When Bart
Starr calls this play, which can be run to the left
or to the right, pads pop against pads and helmets crash into helmets. Above it all you can
hear the grunts and yells of 300-pound giants
crashing into each other like charging buffalo.

This is the famous Lombardi power sweep:

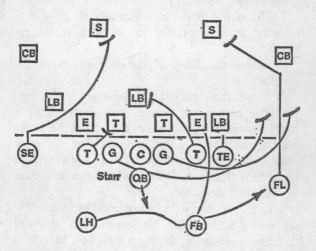

As you can see, the play must be executed
with precise timing. On the snap, the left guard
"pulls" from the line, joining the other guard to
form a wall of thundering blockers. Behind
them Starr hands off to the left halfback
(Hornung in the old days), and the left half-

back follows his blockers on a sweep around end.

Often Starr will call this play when the Packers are ramming toward the goal from inside their opponents' twenty-yard line. It is, as the Packers say, "a money play, the play you use when you want to go in for six."

The play is also effective when the Packers' game plan is to control the ball. Because the ball carrier sweeps wide, each play may use up a minute. Calling such plays, Starr can consume ten minutes on a long touchdown march. When he "goes in for six" he has done more than score a touchdown. He has:

1. Given the opposing quarterback only five minutes in the quarter to score a matching touchdown.

2. Given the Packers' defense a ten-minute breather.

3. Tired the opposition's defense. If the opposing quarterback panics and throws three long passes trying to even the score, he must punt if the passes fail. Then, with only a minute's rest, the opposing defense must trudge back onto the field. Starr loves to run and pass against tired defenses.

Like all quarterbacks, Starr huddles frequently on the sideline with his coach and assistant coaches. Sometimes, during a time out, Starr will trot to the sideline to talk to Lombardi.

"This is done mainly to collect our thoughts," says Starr. "We may have run a play once or twice that has failed. Now I may want to try it again. It's helpful to get the chance to ask Coach Lombardi what he thinks about calling the play — especially when you know that if you call that play, it could mean the difference between winning and losing."

Sometimes, though, even a conference with the coach doesn't help. In one game in 1961 against the Vikings, the Packers drew three straight fifteen-yard penalties. Suddenly Starr had to decide what play to call on third down and a whopping fifty yards to go, the ball deep in his own territory.

What to do? Starr stared blankly at his teammates. Then he turned to look at Lombardi on the sideline.

"Lombardi," says Starr, "just shrugged. He was stumped, too."

12

Bart Starr at Home:
"Not a Mean Word"

BART STARR WALKED up the steps of his home in the quiet Chateau-Liberty section of Green Bay. If Bart had turned, he could have seen — a half mile away — the stadium where the Packers play on Sundays in the fall and winter. But now this was a warm, sunny day in spring.

Bart's son, Bart, Jr., ran across the lawn to greet his father, coming home from a lunch in downtown Green Bay. "Where's Paul Hornung?" said Bart, Jr.

"He couldn't come," said Bart, smiling. Hornung had been in Green Bay to visit old friends. "Paul will come later."

Bart turned to a friend. "Paul Hornung is my son's favorite ballplayer," said Bart. "He'll cheer when I complete a pass, but you should hear him yell when Paul breaks loose on a long run."

Inside the house Bart's wife, Cherry, was feeding their infant son, Brett. "Cherry deserves a hand for what success I've had," Bart was saying. "In those days when we were losing, I'd bring my problems home with me. I'm lucky she understood."

One spring day Len Wagner, a sportswriter for the Green Bay *Press-Gazette*, interviewed some of Bart's neighbors. To these people, Wagner discovered, Bart Starr is simply the man who lives across the street.

"He's accepted here as a neighbor, not as a celebrity," said Robert Stewart. "We'd hate to lose him as a neighbor."

"Of course we know who he is," said Mrs. Marshall Williamson. "But we don't think of him that way. The Starrs are no different from any other neighbors. They're just real fine people."

To Bart Starr's neighbors, wrote Wagner, "He's the guy who, along with his wife, joins the neighborhood gang for a summer Sunday afternoon picnic. He's the guy who offers you the use of his lawn tools when you find yourself confronted with a sticky project. He's the guy who calls to see if your daughter can baby-sit Saturday night."

Robert Stewart and his famous neighbor occasionally stop on the street, or meet in their living rooms, to have long talks. "I've had a couple of real serious talks with Bart," Stewart was saying on this spring day. "I wouldn't want to divulge what we talked about, but he has a deep feeling of wanting to help others, whether it is a teammate on the football field or just some people who may be in unfortunate circumstances. He's asked to contribute to an awful lot of things, and I think he does to ninety-nine per cent of them . . . just because he sincerely wants to be helpful."

All the boys in the neighborhood, of course, know who Bart Starr is. During the football season they watch him on television or from the

stands, cheering as he throws passes and steers
the Packers toward the goal line. But when the
football season is over, says Mrs. Williamson,
"he's just Mr. Starr" to the children of the neighborhood.

Occasionally Bart will invite his son and his
friends to jump into the Starrs' stationwagon.
"Where do you want to go?" Bart asks.

"To McDonald's," the kids holler.

"O.K.," says Bart, grinning. And he starts up
the car, driving the gang to a hamburger stand
for all the malts and burgers they can stow
away, paying the check himself, of course.

On some rainy days Bart may drive the boys
to the local YMCA to shoot basketballs. On
summer evenings Bart often joins the boys in a
game of basketball. The game is played on the
driveway, the backboard and hoop attached to
the roof of the garage.

On other evenings Bart joins some of his
neighbors on the sidewalk for conversation. The
talk is seldom of football. "We just don't talk
football because we figure that everybody that
approaches Bart wants to talk football," says
Robert Stewart. "We talk about our lawn and
the neighborhood and the city, things like that."

During the snowy winter months in frigid
Green Bay, a number of the neighbors call on
Bart for use of his snowblower. "My son," says
Stewart, "usually takes care of Bart's sidewalk
during the winter. And then Bart lets him bring
his snowblower over here and take care of our
walk right away."

On this spring day, Bart tossed a basketball
with Bart, Jr., and two of his friends, Steve Cris-
pigna and Bobbie Stewart. Then he had to leave

for a meeting of the Green Bay Downtown Re-
development Authority. He is a member of the
Authority, which is working to spruce up the
downtown area of Green Bay. Part of Bart's work
includes calling on officials of companies, inviting
them to help the Authority.

After his meeting with the Authority, Bart visited the Reverend Roger Bourland, pastor of the
First Methodist Church. Bart is an active First
Methodist parishioner and a member of the
church's governing board.

"He is really one of the finest Christian gentle-
men I have known," the minister was telling
someone after Bart left. "He is humble, but at the
same time dynamic and exciting. One of his
greatest characteristics is that he does so much
for people in a personal way with his time,
talent, and money. And most of them don't
know that he is responsible.

"He has received many awards and rewards
this year and in past years, but the best ones
have been inner rewards that no one knows
about.

"He has been very influential in bringing
many of the Packers to church services. And he
and Bill Curry and Carroll Dale have taken up
providing devotions for the Protestant boys on
the team when they are on the road. Breakfast
for the team is usually about 9 o'clock and there
aren't many Protestant services in churches before that time. So the boys hold devotions in
one of their rooms."

After leaving the Reverend Bourland, Bart
conferred for a while with an official of Rawhide
Camp. This is a camp for boys from poor or de-
linquent homes who need help. Bart has long

been interested in the camp, and he is now a member of the Rawhide Advisory Board. He is chairman of fund drives, frequently making speeches to raise more money for Camp Rawhide.

It was nearly six o'clock in the evening when Bart steered his stationwagon into the Starr driveway. After dinner with Cherry and his two sons, he tugged out a lawn mower from the garage to make a neat green lawn even neater looking. After mowing for awhile, he stopped to chat with a neighbor, Len Kielgas, with whom he plays golf.

All his life — in high school, college, and in Green Bay — Bart has been interested in sports. All kinds of sports. In high school, when he wasn't playing football, he was running around the track. In college he shot basketballs and hit baseballs. Away from classes he tramped fields, gun in hand, to bang away at high-flying geese or quick-running deer.

But of all those sports, next to football, Bart likes golf the best. He shoots in the low eighties, making him an eight-handicap golfer at the club near Green Bay where he plays. A day earlier Len Kielgas had been showing Bart how he hit short chip shots.

"Let me see how you hit that shot again, Len," said Bart, who was dressed in a white turtleneck sweater and a golfer's cardigan.

"Sure," said Len. He dropped a ball on the lawn. He drew back his nine-iron and chipped a shot a few feet. "The important thing," Len was saying, "is keeping your arm straight as you draw back the club."

Bart watched, his face as intent as when

Coach Lombardi is showing a new play. He was a good golfer, but now — watching Len — he was trying to learn to be a better golfer.

From golf the talk switched to a party one of the neighbors was having at his home the next evening. Throughout the year Bart and his neighbors hold parties. Each July Fourth they have a picnic in someone's backyard, the enticing odor of frying hot dogs and hamburgers floating across the lawns.

"Well," said Len, "I guess we'll see you and Cherry at the party tomorrow night."

"We'll be there," said Bart. He said good-by to Len and went into his home to change into a business suit. This evening he was going to speak to a meeting of Cub Scouts.

At the meeting Bart Starr told the scouts about the kinds of things he believes in. They are the beliefs on which he has built his life.

"Always play to win," said Starr. "Winning may not be everything, but the effort put forth to win *is everything*.

"Any game played is worth striving to win. Winning often demands sacrifice. If not, the game wasn't too important."

"Winning requires teamwork. And winning teamwork, of course, requires that each member perform his individual assignment to the very best of his ability.

"The winning effort, winning teamwork, a winning performance — they all require proper instruction. Listen, learn, and *follow instructions*. Only then can you turn in the winning performance."

The winningest quarterback of all time said

thank you, and he sat down, the Cub Scouts applauding.

After the meeting ended, his neighbor, Robert Stewart, looked across the room at Starr. "Bart is awfully sincere," he said. "He means what he says, exactly what he says. His sincerity really came out in front of these scouts."

Stewart paused, this man who knows Bart Starr so well, this man who has lived a few feet from him for years. "I'll tell you this," said Bart Starr's close friend and neighbor. "I don't think you could find a mean word in our neighborhood about Bart Starr."

13

The Only Place To Be

STARR LOOKED AT THE headlines. On the table in front of him, his meal was turning cold. Bart put down the newspaper, his face grim. "Poor Paul," he said. "What a tough break."

The black headline on the newspaper told why Starr looked grim:

NFL SUSPENDS HORNUNG

During the 1962 season, Paul Hornung had bet on NFL games. He had never bet on his own team. He had never bet on a game in which he was playing. But in every player's contract there is a rule which, in effect, states: "Don't bet on games."

Hornung had broken that rule. The NFL commissioner, Pete Rozelle, suspended Paul for the 1963 season. Hornung said he knew he had done wrong. He hoped his teammates and the public would forgive him.

"People," said Bart, "think Paul is a wild-living guy. Instead he is a real fine person. I ought to know. I have had the locker next to him for six years.

"Now people are going to find out just how fine a person Paul is. He made a foolish mistake. He has said he was sorry. He will come back to be an even greater football player."

A reporter phoned. How would the loss of Hornung affect the Packers in the 1963 season?

"We face a big challenge," said Starr. "No club ever has won the championship three times in a row. Coach Lombardi just has to point out the challenge to us. He knows how much we want to be the first team to win three titles in a row."

In their preseason games, the Packers showed how much they wanted to win that third NFL championship. After losing to the College All-Stars, 20-17, the Packers swept by five NFL opponents. In their game against the Bears, they crushed George Halas' Monsters, 26-7. Trotting off the field, the Packers thought they had no reason to worry about the Bears blocking their way to that third title.

Actually the Packers had good reason to worry about the Bears.

The two teams clashed again on Opening Day at Green Bay's City Stadium. During the preseason games, the Bears had assembled four fast pass defenders — Bennie McRae, Dave Whitsell, Richie Petitbon, and Roosevelt Taylor.

These four would surprise NFL passers in the 1963 season. With the quick hands of pickpockets and the speed of cats, they batted down passes as they floated into the hands of receivers.

On this Opening Day against Green Bay, they

batted down one Starr pass after another — and four they intercepted.

Four interceptions! After that fourth interception, Starr trotted off the field, shaking his head. In the entire previous season, only nine of his passes were intercepted. Already, in less than an hour of the new season, the Bears had intercepted almost half that many.

The Bear offense was a wheezy, chug-chug-chugging tin lizzy, but it scored a touchdown and a field goal. Starr could never get the sleek Green Bay machine to purr and the Bears went off 10-3 winners.

That one defeat didn't worry the Packers. There were, after all, thirteen games left in the season. And, as usual, the Packers worried more about the Colts than they did about the Bears.

Two weeks later the Packers faced the Colts and Johnny Unitas. At the start of the fourth period, the Colts led the Packers, 17-14. Then came one of those breaks that smart quarterbacks turn into touchdowns.

Taking the snap from center, Starr turned and handed off to Jim Taylor. A Colt hit Taylor and the ball leaped out of Jim's arms.

"Fumble! Fumble!" yelled the Colts, scrambling for the ball.

Starr turned and saw the ball hopping toward him. He reached out one hand and scooped up the ball.

"Look out! Pass! Pass!" yelled the Colts.

Starr, thinking fast, was running to his right and looking downfield. Out there, left all alone by the Colts after the fumble, was Boyd Dowler. Starr lined the ball into Dowler's arms and

the rangy receiver scooted thirty-five yards into
the end zone. That put Green Bay ahead, 21-17,
and the Packers went on to win, 31-20.

But that afternoon the Bears also won. The
two teams roared through the first half of the
season, the Bears still leading by a game. Then
the weak 49ers upset the Bears while the Packers beat the Cardinals. Now the two teams were
tied.

Victory over the Cardinals had come at a high
price for the Packers. In the game Starr's right
hand was broken. But No. Two Packer quarterback John Roach filled in for Starr the next week
and led them to a 34-20 victory over the Colts.

Two weeks later the Packers and Bears were
still tied as they lined up for a head-to-head
match at Wrigley Field in Chicago, some forty-
nine thousand Bear fans shrieking for a Monster victory. The four fleet Bear pass defenders
batted down John Roach's passes. The Bears
won, 26-7.

The Packers did not lose a game the rest of
the season, Bart Starr coming back the following Sunday to lead them the rest of the way.
But up to the last Sunday, the Bears also did
not lose a game. On the last weekend of the season, the Packers defeated San Francisco.

In the Packers' clubhouse after the game, the
players were shouting, "Come on, Detroit
Lions."

The next day the Bears were playing the
Lions. If the Lions won, the Packers and the
Bears would be tied. There would be a playoff
game, and the Packers would still have a chance
for that third straight National Football League
championship.

That next day, a Sunday, the Packer players and their fans in Green Bay sat next to TV sets, watching the Lions battle the Bears. Midway through the fourth period, the Lions were behind by only three points, 17-14, and now they were marching toward the Bears' goal line.

"C'mon, you Lions," growled a Packer player, pacing in front of his TV set. Starr looked at the screen, silent, a grim expression on his face.

He watched the Lion quarterback, Earl Morrall, fading back to pass. Morrall threw. "He's got a receiver open," yelled a Packer, watching the TV screen.

Then, as he had done all season long, the Bears' Dave Whitsell whirled out of nowhere. He leaped high into the air to intercept the pass. He twisted away from a Lion tackler and sprinted thirty-nine yards downfield into the end zone.

The Packers stared at the TV screen, openmouthed.

Sixty seconds later the gun sounded. The Bears had won. They were Western Conference champions. The Packers, three years the Western champions and two years the NFL champions, had been dethroned.

Starr slowly got up from the chair and turned off the TV set. "Look," he said later. "We had two chances at the Bears and they beat us both times. They deserve to be champions."

The Bears went on to become 1963 NFL champions, beating the New York Giants, 14-10.

At the start of the 1964 season, most experts said: "Look for Green Bay and Baltimore to fight it out in the West." The experts would prove to be right.

The Packers started the 1964 season with Paul Hornung back, released from his suspension. In their opening game, the Packers avenged those two 1963 losses to the Bears. They beat the Monsters, 23-12, with Hornung scoring eleven of the points and Bart Starr throwing two touchdown passes over the Chicago pass defenders.

But the following week, the Colts and Johnny Unitas beat Starr and the Packers, 21-20, Paul Hornung missing the extra-point kick that would have tied the score.

After the game some Packer fans grumbled about Hornung. He had kicked a fifty-two-yard field goal a week earlier, but the fans forgot about that. "That year's suspension," said one fan, "has put some rust in Hornung's leg. He can't kick any more."

"Heavens," said Bart Starr, "they forgot how many games Paul has won for us with his kicking. Everyone has a right to miss one."

From that game on, though, the Colts and Johnny Unitas could not be caught. They won the 1964 Western Conference title with a 12-2 record, the Packers finishing second with an 8-5-1 record.

In the spring of 1965, I phoned Vince Lombardi to ask him this question:

"What makes a champion?"

Lombardi laughed. "We're not champions," he said. "So why are you asking me?"

"You were champions three of the past five years in the Western Conference," I replied. "I think that gives you a perfect right to talk of champions."

"Well, all right," said Lombardi, still laughing pleasantly. "I'll say this: A champion is someone like Bart Starr. Even when we have been losing, Bart has never lost his poise. He's always cool out there. That, to me, is the mark of a champion — the kind who plays just as well whether you are losing or whether you are winning."

At the start of the 1965 season, though, Lombardi's voice cracked like a whip as he told the Packers: "This year we are going to be number one. If you don't think we are number one, I don't want you playing for me."

At the beginning of the season, the Packers reeled off four straight victories. Then they flew to Detroit to play the Lions. At the half the Lions led the Packers, 21-3.

In the clubhouse during halftime, each Green Bay player felt anger burning inside him. "We had been badly outplayed in the first half," Starr said later. "This is a game of pride, and in the first half our pride was hurt. Win, lose, or draw, a man has to be able to have pride in what he's doing."

The Packers roared out of the clubhouse for the second half. They blocked ferociously for Starr and suddenly he had all the time to find loose receivers. He cocked his arm and threw a sixty-two-yard pass to Bob Long for one touchdown. A little later he reared back and threw thirty-two yards to Tom Moore for another touchdown. Suddenly the Lions' lead had shrunk to four points, the Packers trailing, 21-17.

Near the end of the third period, the Packers

had the ball on their own twenty-three, third down and two yards to go. As the Packers trotted out of the huddle, the Lions bunched up their defenses, looking to throw back Jim Taylor on a plunge up the middle. The big Detroit crowd screamed, "Hold that line! Hold that line!"

At the snap, Bart turned and faked handing the ball to Taylor. Then he turned and rifled a pass over the middle to Carroll Dale.

"It was a great call," Dale said later. "The Lions came rushing up, looking for the plunge by Taylor. The cornerback rushed right by me. When he did, I took off downfield. I didn't make a great catch. Bart put it right there."

The big end caught Bart's pass all alone and ran seventy-seven yards for another Packer touchdown — the third of the third period. Now the Packers led, 24-21.

In the fourth period, Starr ran around end for four yards to score another touchdown. A few minutes later the gun sounded, ending the game, and the stunned Lions walked off the field, 31-21 losers.

In the clubhouse big Lion tackle Alex Karras slumped on a stool. "There was no way," he said, "we could lose after being ahead, 21-3, at the half. I can't believe it. That Starr is really something."

In the Packers' clubhouse, reporters questioned Lombardi. Had he ordered that risky third-down pass to Carroll Dale?

"No, sir," he said emphatically. "Starr is always doing the unexpected. I'd say that was the twenty-eighth time in the last seven years that Starr has crossed up a defense with that call.

And seven of those times he has crossed them up for a touchdown."

Standing in front of a mirror, Starr was knotting his tie. One end of the tie came out too long. Patiently, he untied the knot and began to tie it again, slowly and carefully. Someone asked him about the pass to Dale. "Oh," he said, "we've had success with that play many times before. There was nothing new about it."

"But it was so unexpected," said the reporter, who covered the Lions and, as a result, didn't get to see Starr too often. "I mean, you're supposed to be so careful, so conservative. That was a real daring call."

"Well," said Starr, smiling, "every once in awhile I like to fool 'em." And he laughed.

Down the stretch of the 1965 season, the Packers struggled to hold off the challenge of the Baltimore Colts for the top spot in the Western Conference. But on the last day of the season, the lowly San Francisco 49ers sprang an upset. They tied the Packers, 24-24. That put the Packers in a tie with the Colts. On the next Sunday the Colts and Packers would meet in a playoff for the Western Conference title.

Before the game, few people thought the Colts had much chance to win. The legendary Johnny Unitas was on crutches, his leg injured, and wouldn't be able to play. The Colts' No. Two quarterback, Gary Cuozzo, had his throwing arm in a sling. He couldn't play. Desperate, Baltimore inserted Tom Matte, a halfback, at quarterback. Since Matte couldn't pass, the Colts were forced to use only running plays.

But moments after the opening kickoff, a freak play seemed to even up the game. On the first play from scrimmage, Starr ran back to pass. He threw a short spiral to end Bill Anderson, who caught the ball on the sideline and was hit. The ball bounced out of Anderson's arms.

The Colts' Don Shinnick scooped up the ball on the Packer twenty-five and raced down the sideline, two blockers lumbering in front of him. The only Packer in his path to the goal: Bart Starr.

"I didn't see what happened after I threw the ball," Starr said after the game. "The next thing I knew, Shinnick was coming down the sideline with the ball and a couple of blockers in front of him.

"I didn't think I had much chance to tackle him. But I thought if I could take out the blockers, someone else would get him before he scored."

Starr ran into the huge blockers. They trampled over him. Shinnick ran into the end zone untouched. The Colts led, 7-0. And the Packers' No. One quarterback was writhing on the ground, clutching his side.

Starr's ribs were damaged. He was helped, limping and holding his side, to the Packers' bench. There he tried to throw a football, but he couldn't lift his right arm above his shoulder. Into the game went the Packers' No. Two quarterback, Zeke Bratkowski.

Zeke, as usual, was ready. "He and I think alike," Starr once said. "He often comes to my house and we will sit in the basement, looking at movies of the defenses we're likely to see the next week. Then, on a blackboard, I'll sketch a defense and say: 'What play would you call against this defense?'

"Zeke will pop out an answer. That's what you must be able to do — have the play on the tip of your tongue. On the line of scrimmage there isn't much time for thinking when you see a new defense and have to call an automatic. Then Zeke will sketch a defense on the blackboard and I'll call a play against it. You'd be surprised how often we call the same play."

In this game Zeke called Bart Starr kind of plays. He brought the Packers back from a 10-0 halftime disadvantage to a 10-10 tie. Then, in sudden-death overtime, Zeke steered the Packers to the Colt twenty-five yard line. From there Don Chandler stepped back to try a field goal.

The big Green Bay crowd stood, hushed, as the two teams lined up, the Packers' center crouching over the ball, Zeke kneeling to take the snap and set down the ball.

Back came the ball from center. Zeke set it down. Chandler stepped forward, his foot swinging into the ball.

Boom! Up went the ball. The players turned to watch it float, end over end, through the early-evening dusk toward those white goal posts.

The referee's arms shot high in the air. The kick was good! The Packers had won, 13-10. The Packers were Western Conference champions.

The Green Bay players rushed off the field, shaking hands, clapping each other on the backs. Bart Starr grabbed Zeke Bratkowski, and there were tears in Bart's eyes. "You were great, buddy," said Bart. "I'm so proud of you, really proud."

Now it was a week later — the Sunday of the 1965 championship game. Out on the field the Cleveland Browns warmed up to face the Packers. Up in the press box a reporter asked: "Has Lombardi said who will start — Bratkowski or Starr?"

"He said he'd wait until game time," said another writer. "He wants to see if Bart can throw."

Bart could throw. He started for the Packers. On the first play of the game, Bart scanned the Cleveland defense. He knew, from films, that the Browns are willing to give up short passes. Cleveland defenders usually hang deep to protect against the long bomb.

Now, watching the defense, Bart saw the defenders were hanging deep, as expected. He threw a short pass. *Complete!* And another. *Complete!*

Then Starr sent Carroll Dale out to the left. Starr pumped to throw. In rushed the Cleveland defender, figuring to pick off another one of those short passes.

There was no pass. Bart still had the ball. And now Carroll Dale had hooked behind the defender and was racing downfield, all alone. High into the air arched Bart's pass. Dale caught it on the run and raced forty-seven yards for a touchdown to put the Packers ahead, 7-0.

For the rest of the game, the Cleveland defense hung deep. It had been burned once; it wouldn't be burned twice. So Starr completed short pass after short pass. And he sent Jim Taylor and Paul Hornung bursting through the thinned-out defense for ten- and twenty-yard gains. Scoring slowly and methodically, the

Packers were never in serious trouble. They led 13-12 at the half, 20-12 after three periods, and they won, 23-12.

"I knew after the first period," said Paul Hornung, "that this was 1962 again."

1962! That was the last time the Packers had won an NFL championship. Now it was 1965 and the Packers were sweeping into the clubhouse, champions again!

"It feels great," said giant Jerry Kramer. "This is greater than 1961 and 1962. I wasn't old enough in 1961 and 1962 to know how much this can mean."

Starr slumped on a stool, sweat and grass stains streaking his face. He looked up at a writer. "This is the best win I've ever had," he said. "Everything was so hard all season long. The games against the Colts and the Bears, the playoff against the Colts. Everything."

He looked around this room of shouting, happy champions. "This is the only place to be," he said with a tired smile. "To be with winners."

14

"A Success at Anything in Life"

ZEKE WAS TIPTOEING up on Bart Starr. All the Packers saw what was happening, and they were trying to stop from laughing. It was near the end of a Packer practice session.

Zeke scooped up some muddy water from the playing field, holding it carefully in his palm. In front of him, crouched over the center, Starr was barking signals.

"Thirty-eight, twenty-four . . ." yelled Starr, "sixty-two . . . *Yow!*"

Zeke had dropped the cold, slimy water on the back of Bart's neck and now it was oozing down his spine. Bart had jumped a half a foot off the ground. The Packers burst out laughing.

Bart turned, his hand reaching back to wipe the water off. "You son of a gun," he said to his pal, Zeke. There was a sheepish grin on Bart's face.

Zeke shook, he was laughing so hard. Bart turned to someone who had seen what had happened. "Zeke does that all the time," said Starr. "You'd swear someone had sneezed all over you."

A little later, the practice finished, Starr relaxed on the rubbing table in the Green Bay trainer's room. This was near the end of the 1966 season. The official statistics for the season showed that Bart Starr was the league's leading passer.

"You're back on top again," a reporter said to Starr. "You were the league's leading passer in 1962 and 1964. Now you're the leader again in 1966."

"I'll tell you," said Starr. "It's great to be the top passer. But on this ball club, individual performances don't mean a thing. Corny as it may sound, we're a *team*. We're honestly not concerned with personal images."

Right now, on this next to last weekend of the 1966 season, the Packers were concerned about stopping the Baltimore Colts. If the Packers could beat the Colts, they would win the Western Conference title — their second straight and their fifth in seven years.

Two days before the game, Lombardi flew the squad to Gaithersburg, Maryland, a small town not far from Baltimore. After dinner, Lombardi called a meeting of the offense. Standing in front of a blackboard, Lombardi showed the team the plays he wanted Starr to call when the Packers stood within the ten-yard line.

After the meeting, Starr strolled back to his motel room. He was wearing a beige cardigan and a white turtleneck polo shirt. "I feel great," he told writer Dave Wolf. "Maybe it's the weather but I feel ready now for the Colts. Waiting can be the worst part of this game."

In his room the phone rang. Starr picked up the receiver. "I've got some inside dope on the

Colts' defense," said the caller. And he mentioned something he had seen during the Colt game the previous week.

"Well, thanks," said Starr, smiling. "I'll mention that and the coaches will check it on the films. If they spot anything I'm sure they'll alert us. I appreciate your calling and we hope you continue to root for us."

The next day the team left by bus for their hotel in Baltimore. On the bus, dressed in a green Packer blazer, Starr watched Paul Hornung do card tricks. That night he sat down to a seafood dinner with Jim Taylor and Zeke Bratkowski.

The next morning he awoke with that shaky feeling he always has on game days. "I'm nervous," he said. "I'm nervous before every game."

Yet, in the clubhouse, he was Bart the Cool, walking from stall to stall, patting each player on the back. He was like an army captain getting his men ready to storm a fort.

A little later, the crowd roaring, the game began. The first time Green Bay had the ball, Bart decided to try a short pass over the middle. From what he had seen of the Colt defense in films, he had a hunch a receiver who cut into the middle would be free.

The ball was on the Colts' forty-two. Bart took the snap, angled back, and threw a clothesline pass to Elijah Pitts as he cut over the middle at the twenty-five. Pitts snared the pass and, as Starr had figured, he was all alone. Pitts ran into the end zone and the Packers led, 7-0.

The Colts fought back to take a 10-7 lead. Late in the first half, Bart ran back to pass. A big Colt tackler flattened him. Bart got up dizzy, his legs unsteady. But he stayed in the game, and three more times in the half he was bounced to the ground by the fierce Baltimore pass rush.

"He never complains out there," a teammate said on the bench. "We respect him for that."

The half ended with the Colts still ahead, 10-7. On the sideline, warming up for the second half, Bart tried to throw a pass and a sudden pain knifed through his ribs. "Zeke," he said to his buddy, "you'd better get ready."

Again Zeke ran into a game to replace his pal, Bart Starr. And in the fourth period, with the sureness of a Starr, Zeke passed and ran the Packers into the Colts' end zone. The Packers led, 14-10, with only a few minutes remaining in the game.

The Colts stormed back, Johnny Unitas' magic moving the team swiftly upfield. But inside the Packers' twenty-yard line, Unitas tried to run and was hit from the blind side by a Packer tackler. The ball flew out of Johnny's hands, and a Packer tumbled on the ball. Moments later the gun roared.

The Packers were winners! The Packers were Western Conference champions!

Ahead was a battle with the Dallas Cowboys for the NFL championship — and, in this year of 1966, something new.

The something new: The first Super Bowl game, a clash with the champions of the American Football League. Each player on the winning team in the Super Bowl would get $15,000.

To get into the Super Bowl, though, the Packers had to beat the Cowboys. And they had to beat the Cowboys at home. The 1966 National

Football League championship game would be
played in the Cotton Bowl at Dallas.

An hour before the game, some seventy-two
thousand Texans and a handful of Green Bay
rooters jammed the stands. "Now you'll see
football Texas style," the Cowboy rooters told
the Green Bay fans. "Now your conservative Mr.
Bart Starr is going to see a gambling quarterback."

The gambling quarterback was Don Meredith, the Dallas passer who had been throwing
high, wide, and handsome this 1966 season. In
this game, though, the fans were going to see
some gambling by the conservative Mr. Bart
Starr.

Early in the game, Starr carefully guided the
Packers to the seventeen. The Dallas defense
jammed up its line, figuring Starr would be careful so early in the game.

When Starr saw the defense was looking for a
run, he faded back. Now the Dallas fans were
seeing that Mr. Conservative could also be a
gambler. He threw an arching spiral that Elijah
Pitts snatched at the goal line. Pitts squirmed
by two tacklers into the end zone and Green
Bay led, 7-0.

On the kickoff Dallas' Mel Renfro fumbled
the ball. A Packer picked up the bouncing ball
and galloped into the end zone. Green Bay
kicked the extra point again and led, 14-0.

Many people, watching on TV, figured the
Packers were going to run away with this game
but they were to be surprised. This game would
go down to the last minute as one of the closest
and most thrilling of all NFL championship
games.

Within a few minutes, in fact, the Cowboys had stormed back to tie the game, 14-14. In the second period, Starr threw a soaring spiral deep to Carroll Dale. Up for the ball went the tall Dale and the lean Dallas defender, Cornell Green.

But Green leaped too soon. He started downward, helpless, his fingers clawing the air, as the ball arched into the hands of Dale. The big receiver latched onto the ball and scampered into the end zone — a daring forty-nine-yard touchdown pass that put the Packers ahead, 21-14.

Still the proud Cowboys wouldn't quit. They kicked a field goal and at the half, the Green Bay lead was down to four points, 21-17.

Early in the third period Dallas kicked another field goal: Green Bay 21, Dallas 20.

The fans roaring, Bart Starr guided the Packers to the Dallas sixteen. Again the Cowboys figured the conservative Starr wouldn't pass, not in a game this close, not when he was only sixteen yards from the end zone. But again Starr gambled, dancing back and lining a spiral into the arms of Boyd Dowler. Dowler tumbled into the end zone and Green Bay now had a breathing-room kind of lead, 28-20.

By now Dallas realized that Starr's game plan was a passing game. (He had a good reason to pass; for several weeks the Green Bay rushing game had been sputtering badly.) Knowing Starr was going to pass, the Cowboys began to blitz — rushing in cornerbacks or safetymen to try to flatten Starr before he could get the ball away.

Standing in his pocket, Starr was as cool as a rifleman facing a cavalry charge. Ignoring the

blitzers, he quickly zipped passes into the arms
of his receivers.

The ball was on the Green Bay forty-three,
third down and nineteen yards to go. *Zip!*
Starr threw to Marv Fleming for twenty-four
yards and a first down.

Two plays later the ball was on the Dallas
thirty-five, third down and twelve yards to go.
Zip! Starr threw to Jim Taylor for sixteen yards
and another first down. On the next third-down
play, the ball was on the Dallas twenty-eight and
the Packers had to pick up nineteen yards. In
the huddle Starr called a pass play. As the team
broke from the huddle, end Max McGee whispered to Starr: "Can I change my pattern a little?"

Starr nodded. He took the ball and ran back,
watching McGee run the pattern. Again he was
gambling, taking a chance he wouldn't be tackled on this big third-down play while he waited
for McGee to switch the pattern.

Thwack! A Dallas blitzer smacked into a
blocker next to Starr. The lineman swung an
arm at Starr, but Bart ducked.

Now! Starr saw McGee switch the pattern
and gain a step on the man covering him. Still
calm and cool, Starr cocked and threw, spiral-
ing a pass that led McGee perfectly. The ball
sailed into Max's hands near the end zone and
McGee, all alone, skipped across the goal line.
Green Bay now led, 34-20, and there were less
than six minutes to play.

Still Dallas wouldn't quit. Inspired by their
roaring fans, the Cowboys quickly scored to
trail by only a touchdown, 34-27. One more

touchdown would tie the game and send it into sudden-death overtime.

Minutes later the Cowboys were within two yards of a tie. The ball was on the Green Bay two, first down and two to go for the tying touchdown. There was a minute and fifty-two seconds left to play, time enough to go two scant yards.

On the first play Dan Reeves plunged to the one, the Green Bay line swaying and then holding. "We knew we could stop them," Green Bay linebacker Lee Roy Coffey said later. "We got together in the defensive huddle and we said we couldn't let the offensive team down. Bart Starr had called such a beautiful game."

Dallas lined up, second and one to go. As Meredith called the signals, a tense Dallas lineman jumped off-side. The referee's whistle blew. Dallas was penalized five yards back to the six.

With second down and six to go, Meredith threw a pass that fell incomplete, Dan Reeves bobbling the ball. On third down Meredith threw complete to end Pettis Norman, a gang of Packers burying Norman on the two.

Now it was fourth down with two yards to go for the tying touchdown. Roaring filled the Cotton Bowl as Dallas came up to the line of scrimmage. From the sideline, fists clenched, Bart Starr watched, tense.

Meredith took the snap from center and rolled to his right. At the sideline he saw he couldn't run by Green Bay's big Dave Robinson. Meredith threw a hasty, wobbly pass, hoping a Dallas receiver would run under the ball in the end zone. In the end zone, however, Packer safetyman Tom Brown ran under the ball, clasping it to his chest and falling to the ground.

Interception! Green Bay had stopped the Cowboys. On the bench Starr jumped up and down, grabbing the hands of the Packer defense as the players streamed off the field.

Moments later the game ended. The Packers picked up Vince Lombardi and carried him off the field. They were National Football League champions for the second straight year — and now they were on their way to the Super Bowl.

In that 1966 NFL championship game, Starr completed nineteen of twenty-eight passes. Four of them were for touchdowns — four of the five touchdowns Green Bay had scored. And not one of his passes had been intercepted.

On a football field in California, the Packers drilled for the Super Bowl game. Late one evening, after a workout, Starr sat quietly and talked with someone about his remarkable career.

He looked back on a career that began with great promise in a Montgomery high school and on the gridiron of the University of Alabama. It was a career almost snuffed out on a University of Alabama bench and, later, on the playing fields of the National Football League.

Then Vince Lombardi had come to Green Bay. He had turned a quiet, worried quarterback into a cool, confident leader of men. Now, in the warmth of this California night, Starr talked about Lombardi.

"The man's personality rubs off on you," he said. "He is a demanding, driving person who will not settle for second best. When you are around him long enough, you begin to think like him. And, maybe, act like him. You, too, become demanding and driving. You, too, will not settle for second best.

"I used to suffer agonies when I was intercepted. I would let failure fester in me. But not anymore. I learned a lot from coach Lombardi. A couple of years ago I told him I had learned so many lessons playing football for him that I felt I could be a success at anything in life."

A few days later Starr got ready to leave for the Los Angeles Coliseum to play in the Super Bowl — a game the Packers would win, a game that Bart Starr would come out of as its Most Valuable Player.

On the way he met his wife, Cherry. Bart could see that she was very nervous. "Now, now, sweetie," he said, laughing. "Don't worry. I'm the one who has to play. Not you."

Bart laughed, the white teeth showing in the handsome fair face. Then he went laughing toward the Super Bowl, this quarterback who had learned confidence with hard work and a willingness to shrug off disappointment.

This quarterback they now call Bart the Cool.

HIGHLIGHTS OF BART STARR'S CAREER

Bart Starr
Quarterback — Green Bay Packers
No. 15
School: University of Alabama
Born: Montgomery, Alabama, January 9, 1934
Height and Weight: 6′ 1″, 200 pounds

All-American High School player at Sidney Lanier High in Montgomery . . . All-SEC as a freshman at U. of Alabama . . . In 1953 Orange Bowl completed 8 of 12 passes for 93 yards and one touchdown . . . Second best punter in the nation in 1953 . . . Completed 53 out of 119 passes in 1953 for 870 yards and 8 touchdowns . . . Had only 6 intercepted . . . Missed most of 1954 season . . . In 1955 completed 55 of 96 passes for 587 yards and one touchdown . . . Had 9 intercepted.

Drafted by Packers in 17th round in 1956 . . . Broke in under Tobin Rote . . . Shared position with Babe Parilli and Lamar McHan in 1958 and 1959 . . . Regular in 1960 . . . Has won more games than any other quarterback in pro ball . . . 57% completion average over career . . . quarterbacked Packers to Western Conference titles in 1960, 1961, 1962, 1965, and 1966 . . . World titles in 1961, 1962, 1965, and 1966 . . . Has completed highest percentage of passes in career of any other pro quarterback . . . Has lowest percentage of interceptions of any other pro quarterback . . . Holds NFL record of 294 consecutive passes without an interception . . . NFL leading passer in 1962, 1964, and 1966 . . . Most Valuable Player in NFL in 1966 . . . Voted MVP in AFL-NFL Super Bowl 1967 . . . Played in Pro Bowl in 1961, 1962, 1963, and 1966 . . . During off-season does sales promotion . . . Lives in Green Bay, Wisconsin.

SEASON RECORD

Year	Atts	Comp	Yds	Tds	Int	Ave	%
1956	44	24	325	2	3	7.49	54.5
1957	215	117	1489	3	10	6.93	54.4
1958	157	78	875	3	12	5.57	49.7
1959	134	70	972	6	7	7.25	52.2
1960	172	98	1358	4	8	7.90	57.0
1961	295	172	2418	16	16	8.19	58.3
1962	285	178	2438	12	9	8.55	62.5
1963	244	132	1855	15	10	7.60	54.1
1964	272	163	2144	15	4	7.88	59.9
1965	251	140	2055	16	9	8.19	55.8
1966	251	156	2257	14	3	8.99	62.2

NFL CHAMPIONSHIP GAMES

Year	Atts	Comp	%	Yds	Tds	Int
1960	35	21	60.0	178	1	0
1961	17	10	58.8	164	3	0
1962	22	10	45.5	106	0	0
1965	19	10	52.6	147	1	1
1966	28	19	67.9	304	4	0

AFL-NFL SUPER BOWL GAME

1967	23	16	69.6	250	2	1